Mayday
Over the Arctic!

Cover and inside illustrations by Eric Anderson
Cover design by Steve Lanto
Inside design by Aaron Troia

All Scriptures are quoted from the King James Version.

You can obtain additional copies of this book by calling toll-free 1-800-765-6955 or by visiting http://www.adventistbookcenter.com.

Library of Congress Cataloging-in-Publication Data

Nelson-Nelson, Dorothy, 1929-
  Mayday over the Arctic
Dorothy Nelson Nelson.
     p. cm.
  ISBN-13: 978-0-8163-2291-6 (pbk.)
  ISBN-10: 0-8163-2291-0 (pbk.)
  1. Nelson-Nelson, Dorothy, 1929- 2. Survival after airplane accidents, ship-wrecks, etc.—Davis Strait. 3. Missionaries, Medical—Biography. I. Title.
  R722.32.N455 2009
  610.73'49092—dc22
  [B]
                                                                    2008049390

09 10 11 12 13 • 5 4 3 2 1

Readers are excited about *Mayday Over the Arctic!*

"Some wonder if there's really a God who hears and answers prayer—a God who actually cares about people. Dorothy N. Nelson, 'the flying nurse,' a lady I've known for over sixty years, doesn't wonder at all. God has answered her prayers over and over again. Time after time He's done the 'impossible' to help her minister to people in need of both spiritual and physical healing. Read this exciting, faith-building book and be reminded that God is very much alive and keeps His promise: 'Lo, I am with you alway, even unto the end of the world.' "

—Kenneth E. H. Richards, retired writer, producer and associate speaker for the Voice of Prophecy radio broadcast.

"If anyone is looking for a book that will tell not only an honest story but one so gripping that you may lose some sleep before you gasp for the last page, this is it! Dorothy Nelson has been my forever model of a down-to-earth, gracious Christian for many decades. But within that remarkable life, she has shown everyone how to be a remarkable mother and wife, a gifted musician with instruments and songs of her own creativity, a highly committed nurse with many dire situations, a stunning platform lecturer, a creative health lecturer with fresh props that speak in many languages, and, of course, an airplane pilot and instructor in most any plane flying with perhaps the exception of a jet. This book you hold will reveal how everything written above became useful in this Arctic ordeal—she could never have survived without her lifetime of constant, immediate, unshakeable, trusting relationship with her Lord. Trust me, this is the book of the century!"

—Herbert Edgar Douglass, ThD

"The year was 1980 when a miracle of my own bounced me into Weimar's Newstart Lifestyle Center. I soon met Dorothy Nelson on her way to the airport. She urged me to ride with her (so we could talk) and talk we did!

Her vision, her enthusiasm, her warmth and energy intrigued and inspired me. We met briefly over the years from time to time exchanging news, planning projects, finding ways to help each other. This courageous woman dreamed big dreams, but then set about to put them into action. Her dedication, her love of life never failed to lift my often lagging spirit and put me back on track once again.

If you ever wondered what a life totally dedicated to the Lord could look like, be sure to read this story God slowed her down long enough to write!"

—*Aileen Ludington, MD*
Health Educator, Author and Co-founder of
Dr. Hans Diehl's CHIP* Seminars

*Coronary Health Improvement Project

Mayday
Over the Arctic!

Dorothy N. Nelson

Pacific Press® Publishing Association
Nampa, Idaho
Oshawa, Ontario, Canada
www.pacificpress.com

Dedication

To my late husband, Bill:
"Just can't wait to fly with you again!"

To my loving and supportive family:
James, Becky, Richard, Anna, Ken, Lena, Janet, Ken,
Larry, and Dorothy

To eight precious grandchildren who make Grandma's
flying stories literally come alive:
Kimberly, Heidi, Freja, Kenny, Nikki, Soren, Billy, and Tommy

To a young boy, Craig, now grown, who lost his pilot
father before he could learn to fly.

And to all families who have lost loved ones in the challenge of
mission flying.

Preface

Glancing out the window and hearing the call to prayer, I realize I am at what seems to be the farthest possible place from home . . . the other side of the world in Riyadh, Saudi Arabia. It is here by invitation from my son, Richard, and freed from a busy schedule at home that I am now able to tell "the rest of the story." It's a story which has been hidden from public view . . . a very personal one. Sitting here at my computer in Richard's apartment I review the manuscript before me . . . one started soon after my unforgettable experience in the Arctic. Still vivid in memory I call to mind the handwritten pages filling notebook after notebook, scraps of handwritten notes, flight logs, news articles, pictures, telegrams, and diary entries which had been tucked away in a box of memories . . . preserved perhaps for grandchildren to enjoy. Never in print, the experience has ever been on my mind for how can one forget?

Far out in the sand dunes of the Arabian Desert my manuscript followed me; to a nearby neighborhood park I carried chapters for review; and when the grandchildren were sleeping (those precious active boys) I sat at my computer to finish the final pages. Without the insistence and help of family and friends this book might never have been completed: close friend, Audrey Watts, so willing to review and make suggestions; daughter, Janet Penner, and other family members, Anna, Becky, and Lena, kept up communication that wouldn't let me rest—"How's the book coming along?" became a byword in the family. My son, Ken's tireless effort in formatting the book and James' ever ready help with technical problems proved a stimulus to continue. It was son, Richard, at age thirteen, who flew on Pan American flight 811 with baby brother, Jaime, to the Philippines. This made it possible for me to fly our own plane, the twin engine *Piper Aztec* across the Pacific. Thus began the fulfillment of a dream, a missionary flying program to reach distant islands with an aircraft.

There is nothing in this book that I attribute to any special skills or talents on my part. I was a shy little girl with a dream and God responded to that dream in His own way and His own timing. For the opportunities and privileges God has given me, I am deeply grateful. "Christ in the cockpit" has been my constant guide throughout my flying ministry, for without Him, where would I be today?

This experience is my own personal story. It is coming from the soul of one who believes there is a God up there, a heavenly Father, who will soon return to planet Earth to rescue and bring home downed pilots and all others who have chosen to serve under His banner.

My dear husband and flying companion is gone now, but I expect to fly with him again, someday soon. My sincere prayer is that those whose lives have been touched by my experience will desire to be among those hearing that final radio call, "cleared for takeoff."

Foreword

I am very grateful for the pioneering work of the Nelsons and for the work that Dorothy has continued to do as well as members of her family. The books *Ministry of Healing* and *Welfare Ministry* tell us that we need those who are willing to take a risk in soul winning by putting new life into old methods of labor, those who are able to invent new plans and new methods of successful soul winning and health evangelism. I believe that God planted this philosophy and conviction in the hearts of Wilbur and Dorothy Nelson.

As General Conference President in 1981, I was preparing for a city-wide evangelistic meeting in Manila, the capital city of the Philippines. It seemed providential that the Nelsons suggested developing a professional and impressive Health Expo or health fair which would launch the meetings and then continue each evening prior to the meetings themselves. My recollection is so vivid as it met with enthusiastic support and outstanding success. I was an immediate convert to this approach in connection with major city evangelism.

Later while on other appointments in the Philippines, I flew with Dorothy in the *Wings of Health* airplane. This book understandably comes to me with special meaning. Thank you very much, Dorothy, and a sincere tribute for your years of monumental health evangelism. Blessings to you and continued success to the whole family.

Neal C. Wilson
General Conference President
1979–1990

"Pastor J. L. Tucker; one of the early visionary pioneers for promotion and funding mission airplanes through The Quiet Hour; shares the cockpit of the Lake Amphibian *with pilot, Dorothy, as Wilbur Nelson looks on. The* Lake Amphibian *is one of the many aircraft . . . aircraft that have blessed and served untold thousands of people and the Seventh-day Adventist church in its mission of bringing help, hope, and healing with the gospel of Jesus."*

Contents

Introduction

Dorothy Nelson, known by many as "the flying nurse," flew several Quiet Hour planes, including one that went down in the Arctic. To His glory, God preserved her to tell the story.

Dorothy did much for the mission aviation program championed by The Quiet Hour. Over the years, The Quiet Hour funded fifty airplanes to various fields of the world to assist the work of the Seventh-day Adventist church.

I was privileged to fly with her in the *Wings of Health,* a *Twin Bonanza,* dedicated to bringing health, healing, and the good news to the islands of the Philippines.

Through Dorothy's vision and aviation fervor, new areas such as Tawi Tawi were opened to the gospel.

May her visions for aviation continue in the hearts of future mission pilots until every nook and cranny of this world is penetrated with the gospel of Jesus Christ.

Pastor Bill Tucker
President
The Quiet Hour

The versatile land and sea aircraft . . . Lake 1107 Lima

CHAPTER 1
"Aircraft Calling on 121.5"

"Lake One-One-Zero-Seven-Lima. Confirm you are declaring an emergency."

"That's affirmative," I reply mechanically, scarcely believing my own words. My fingers tighten around a cold microphone as I stare at the instrument panel.

Just moments earlier a pilot friend and I had felt comfortable and secure, looking down from our single-engine *Lake Amphibian* upon a frozen world below. We are at the very threshold of the Arctic Circle. It is late afternoon, a crisp, clear day in March. The irregular black shadows of icebergs make a checkerboard of an otherwise all-white wilderness. Limitless ice fields glisten. This part of the planet is starkly beautiful, unearthly, like a moonscape and, we realize, almost as inhospitable. I glance at the OAT (outside air temperature gauge). It reads a frigid forty degrees below zero. Our heater is poor at best, but still, it lessens the cold and we are grateful for it.

It has been several hours since we took off from the snow-swept runway at Frobisher Bay,[1] on a flight originating from

---

1. Frobisher Bay is an inlet of the Labrador Sea in the SE corner of Baffin Island.

Long Beach, California. Refueling stops had been made in Collegedale, Tennessee; Gaithersburg, Maryland; with a final inspection by the FAA (Federal Aviation Administration) in Portland, Maine. It was in Portland that I had a quick drain installed to make it more convenient for oil changes along our route. We had then proceeded on to Moncton, point of entry for Canada, where we cleared customs. As pilot-in-command, I answered necessary questions confirming my understanding of Canadian flight rules. Once cleared, our flight continued on to Goose Bay with a stopover in Fort Chimo, the largest community in Quebec's arctic region.

It was in Fort Chimo that I first experienced the meaning of the term, "raw edges of the far North," a bitter, indescribable cold. Overseeing the refueling of the ferry tanks, I wondered how anyone could survive in such an unearthly atmosphere. My pilot

Pilot friend, Aubrey Kinzer

friend, less prepared for the cold, had hastily retreated to the nearby barracks-style building. I later discovered him with an absorbed group of pilots and crew members of Survair. Aubrey Kinzer was a family friend and experienced pilot-mechanic whom I had asked to accompany me on this transatlantic flight. Although other pilots had been considered, Aubrey's clear thinking and calm manner under stress appealed to me.

With refueling completed, I made my way to the barracks, our shelter for the night. The room assigned me was adjacent to the lounge area and the cot in the corner was a welcome sight. I was tired and hoped to sleep off the biting cold. Soon however the "hangar talk"—tales of Arctic life—began filtering under the door, transporting me to Eskimo igloos and outposts of the far North. Incredible stories . . . incredible pilots!

In the morning, our preflight inspection included the heating of our engine. Two fur-clad mechanics fired up a well-worn heater on

Heating the engine at Fort Chimo

wheels. Warm air was blown through hoses, one to the engine and another into the cockpit. How thankful we were for that twenty-five dollar service. Leaving Fort Chimo, the next leg of our flight will take us across the Davis Strait, lying between Greenland and Baffin Island. This body of water is known for its fierce tides, an area where icebergs drift down out of Baffin Bay. There the weather can be fickle and vicious and I knew we now faced some of the coldest temperatures of the entire flight.

I had looked forward to this part of the trip with keen anticipation and a sense of awe over the mystery of icebergs. I had read about the continent-wide glaciers and the pressure ridges that take shape under the tremendous squeeze from the seas . . . the shifting saltwater platforms as they rumble their way south in the spring of the year. And now I was to be an eager spectator . . . where earth seems to touch heaven and boundaries disappear; where new horizons are formed; where the Northern lights create ever moving tapestries of varied colors. It was to be an unforgettable experience and I was absorbing every moment of it.

The grandeur of Greenland lay before us. From here we would continue to Iceland, flying over the Faroe Islands en route to Stornoway on the Isle of Lewis. Crossing western Europe, we would then proceed through Greece, Turkey, Iran, Pakistan, India, Thailand, and Singapore. The final stops would be Kuching and Brunei before reaching our destination—Manila, Philippines. My husband and two of our sons would be waiting there to meet our plane. The versatile little *Lake Amphibian* would greatly extend the services of MAP (Medical Aviation Programs) in reaching isolated islands. As pilot nurse with MAP I had flown some thirty thousand miles in an aging *Piper Aztec,* one which I had flown across the Pacific. I was eagerly looking forward to the land and sea capabilities of the amphibious aircraft. No longer would remote islanders need to depend on arduous and unpredictable boat trips for emergency medical care. No longer would seriously ill patients be brought to our plane too late to be helped. The seaplane will be able to land on the shores of smaller islands and transport patients quickly for medical care. How grateful I am for such an aircraft! My sincere thanks to the ministry of The Quiet Hour[2] which made this dream a reality, truly an answer to many prayers.

Months of planning had gone into the preparation of this flight. Limited fuel capacity made the distance over water between Pacific islands prohibitive in the *Lake Amphibian.* It was necessary to take the alternate, much longer route through Europe and Asia. Cables had been sent to each country giving expected dates of ar-

---

2. The Quiet Hour is an evangelism, broadcast media, and publishing ministry of the Seventh-day Adventist church.

Lake Amphibian

rival and fuel requirements. A trip to Washington D.C. and a visit with Congresswoman Shirley Pettis, proved a memorable experience.[3] In her office, a large portrait of her husband, the late Jerry Pettis, reminded me of his untimely death in a plane crash near our home in Cherry Valley, California. "You do live dangerously," she whispered, but extended her hands in gracious understanding, sensing my dedication to mission flying.

The moment I had dreamed of, planned for and worked toward had finally arrived. Pencil lines on paper now carved flight paths in the skies as aeronautical charts merged into real places: seas, skies, and lands. Cape Dyer was now more than just a name on a chart as I looked down upon its radar facilities projecting through a blanket of snow and ice.

I capture the silent beauty on film and then turn towards Greenland, the largest island in the world with its spectacular ice-covered peaks. Flying over the island previously in a commercial airliner, I marveled at the magnificent beauty of ice which covers this majestic island. I was eagerly looking forward to this part of our flight.

---

3. Congresswoman Pettis and her husband were friends from California where their outstanding services in Loma Linda were well-recognized and appreciated.

Flying over Cape Dyer

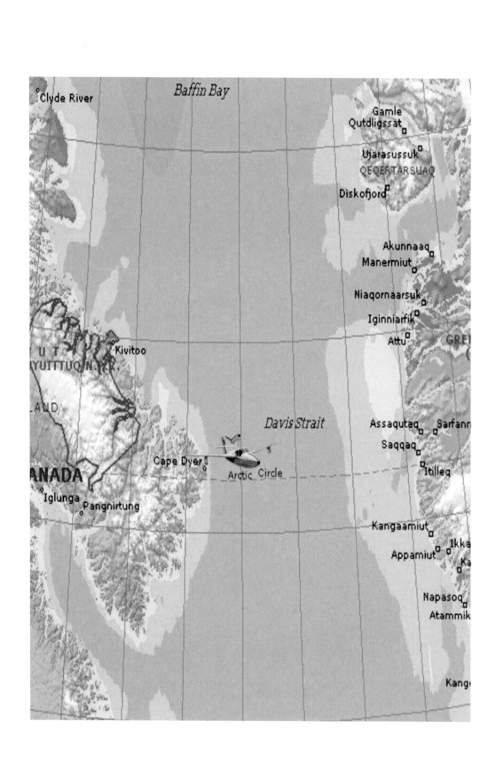

Climbing through 8,000 feet on an instrument flight plan, I had just made a position report which was picked up by an ice patrol aircraft.

"Alpha Zulu," an interested captain radioed. "Let us know if we can be of any assistance."[4]

Little did I realize how much those simple words would mean just moments later.

---

4. The majority of the radio communications reproduced here is the result of a tape recorder continuing to function throughout the transmissions while on the ice floe. Where possible, the precise words as recorded and later transcribed are used (the ever-present "uh" is often omitted for clarity and shown by ellipse).

CHAPTER 2
8,000 Feet and Falling!

The 200-horsepower Lycoming engine had not missed a single beat since our departure. Engine instrument needles remain reassuringly rigid in their normal operating range as I continue to climb to our assigned altitude.

Scanning our instruments, we suddenly notice a flicker of an oil pressure needle. In disbelief we watch the needle waver, drop to the red line, and an instant later settle motionless on zero.

We quickly monitor other gauges. They all remain normal including the oil temperature. Perhaps, yes, perhaps it is only a malfunctioning gauge. We try to reassure ourselves as the engine continues its encouraging drone. I glance at the clock and estimate our time en route. We are sixty-five nautical miles out of Cape Dyer and approximately one third of the way to our next stop . . . Greenland.

I radio our problem and decide to turn back to Cape Dyer where we had seen an airstrip while passing a radar station there.

Forty-five seconds pass and we remain hopeful. The oil temperature gauge continues in the normal range and we begin to breathe easier, encouraged that it's probably a malfunctioning oil pressure gauge. We decide however to continue our return to Cape Dyer.

Suddenly and very abruptly, a shudder, unnerving and sickening, shakes the plane. Then silence. Total silence confirms our worst fears. Our one and only engine has failed. Immediately the nose of the aircraft turns sharply upward and I instinctively push forward on the yoke. With the engine mounted above the fuselage, the *Lake Amphibian* without power points heavenward. In an unavoidable descent, the aircraft now plunges us a thousand feet per minute toward a frozen world below. Stark whiteness gives the feeling of blindness . . . of looking and not seeing. Against this wall of white emerges a long line of accident statistics, ones my friends had warned me about, the risks of flying touching all pilots sooner or later.

I had assured friends and relatives alike that these figures reflect mostly pilot error. Only a small percentage, some 3 percent, are mechanical failures. We are now among that 3 percent.

All systems had been functioning perfectly. What could have gone wrong? A mechanic's forgotten bit of work? Water in the fuel line? Careful pre-flight checks had not revealed any such indications of trouble. I was becoming preoccupied with attempts at diagnosis when the biting wind penetrating the cockpit, wakened me to the challenge of the situation.

We have just eight minutes to find a possible landing site, I remind myself. Straining our eyes for any place suggestive of survival, we suddenly see ahead what appears to be water.

Breaking the monotony of an all white surface ahead is a seventy-five feet wide black channel. Immediately we turn towards the channel and prepare for a possible water landing. It seems the aircraft is in a free fall for which we have no control, other than directing, in its plunge toward the channel. As we approach more closely we search for ripples. What we see startles us! There are no ripples . . . only what appears to be a glass-like glaze of steel. Our inviting black channel is not water after all, but a deceptive death-trap, a layer of ice which, upon contact, could easily slice through the hull of our small aircraft. The decision is made. We will have to turn away . . . away from the channel we felt certain was our only hope of survival. Our altimeter continues to unwind and minutes seem on double time.

We now look intently ahead into what appears to be a closing curtain of gray. I reach for the microphone.

"How thick is the ice?" I question the ice patrol captain monitoring the frequency.

"Uh . . . about twelve inches," he replies.

Fragmented feelings become numb as I watch the altimeter needle plunge through 4,300, 4,200, 4,100 feet. Cold air begins filling the cockpit as our heater, dependent on the engine, is now inoperative. We become captives to the insult of the Arctic air's invasion, a piercing and relentless cold. The plane's pitch attitude without power has changed considerably. I stare ahead. The horizon has taken the form of a series of forbidding ice ridges. We become painfully conscious of the boat-like features of the sea-plane as the aircraft continues its plummet one thousand feet per minute. It seems we are dropping with as much gliding capability as a sinking ship.

Reality soon strikes us with razor-sharp awareness. The loss of our only engine means we are committed to land. There will be no go-arounds, no missed approaches. We also know we have an obstacle course for a runway. No familiar farmer's field or country road, just a frozen sea of white, ruptured by occasional slabs of ice protruding at odd angles over its glistening surface. Our last radio communication provided us with surface winds and as the plane continues to plunge earthward, I feel for the life raft and pull down the life jackets from on top the ferry tank. Fumbling for the straps I put one on. *Why*, I wondered, except it occupied time. Time—that precious commodity so lightly regarded until it runs out. I pass the other life vest to Aubrey. He holds it momentarily, his expression revealing what we both know only too well. A life jacket would only serve to prolong the final few inevitable moments in the icy waters of the Arctic.

Our descent continues. The bone-chilling cold becomes a ruthless invader permeating every corner of our once comfortable cockpit. A sacred silence now prevails as if in respect to the thousand thought processes in operation. *What does one say with only a few remaining minutes to speak . . . to pray?*

Suddenly as if reading my thoughts, Aubrey, now at the controls, breaks the silence. "Dorothy, say a prayer for us both." The

Looking for a place to land

somber tone reflected the hopelessness of the situation, yet it revealed the faith we both had in the existence of Someone in control—that Someone with whom I had been in constant contact.

CHAPTER 3
Touchdown!

Our eyes are now riveted to one small flat area sandwiched between two pressure ridges ahead. Continuing to descend, we soon find ourselves between chunks of ice, frozen monuments in what seems to be one continuous city of ice. Focusing on the altimeter I call out the altitudes—700, 600, 500. We begin to level our descent for a gradual touchdown, a glassy water landing in a *Lake Amphibian* on ice! A landing in white-out conditions as in an instrument approach . . . one this aircraft has done many times under glassy water conditions with my students. We wait. Moments seem light years away.

Suddenly . . . contact! The hull of the aircraft touches the icy surface. Just as suddenly, we become airborne again, a chunk of ice propelling us upward. Then, almost imperceptibly, the aircraft settles back onto the ice. There is no crushing sensation, only a quiet caressing as our *Lake Amphibian* slides along. It seems to gain momentum over the icy surface like one endless toboggan ride, a strange feeling without the braking effect of either water or wheels. Ten- and twelve-foot chunks of ice flash by my window. I watch the wings and wait for one to tip gliderlike,

Touchdown on an ice floe

with a possible ground loop. I watch. I wait. I marvel. The wings do not tip. Someone has retained directional control of a ship we are powerless to stop. We both wait in subdued silence. *When will our toboggan ride end?* I wondered. We continue to slide. Moments seem to stretch into eternity. Then, almost imperceptibly, the aircraft slows, makes a gentle turn, and stops.

We have landed—at the Arctic Circle!

For one brief moment we don't move, affected by the incredible realization we had survived. *We are alive!* It's a moment that instantly locks itself in memory. Unfastening my seatbelt, I throw open the plastic windshield and take a deep breath. It's the last deep breath I ever attempted as the bitter cold felt like fire in my lungs.

Climbing out of the aircraft onto the ice, I drop to my knees. "Oh, thank You, heavenly Father!"

We are alive! Alive in the Arctic! Alive on an ice floe!

Words cannot express the depth of feeling at that moment . . . unspeakable joy and gratitude. Aubrey and I both knew that a Divine Presence had landed our stricken ship.

My blood, perhaps thinned from years of living in the tropics, must have jelled almost instantly. I begin to move as if under water, to breathe as if afraid of the air, to walk as if in space. I discover that normal functions are taking much longer to perform. Items in the aircraft take on new and strange characteristics. My usually flexible camera strap becomes stiff and brittle and a plastic plotter snaps in my fingers. Even the extreme Montana winters I experienced as a child had not prepared me for such unbelievable conditions.

Reaching back into the aircraft, I set about to make contact with the outside world. Oh, the miracle of radio, that wireless wonder, which makes the unreachable reachable, the distant near, the unseen heard, whether alone on an ice floe or in the crowded airspace of a major airport. The ability to reach beyond the confines of a cockpit fills me with gratitude. *Thank you, Marconi.*

We reach for that miracle. "Uh. . . Lake 1107 Lima . . . calling aircrafts monitoring 121.5."

"OK . . . we're Alpha Zulu," a familiar and reassuring voice replies. "We're on 121.5 and we're just about coming up to your position very shortly. We have advised Frobisher and they are aware of it. As soon as we have our position we'll pass on the co-ordinates to Frobisher Bay. Over."

The voice was that of the same captain, Alpha Zulu, who previously had offered help should we need it. How comforting to hear that voice again!

"OK . . . we were on a pretty direct line from Cape Dyer to Sondestrom. . . when we lost the oil."

"OK . . . fine . . . and confirm once again everyone is OK"

"Uh . . . yes, we rode it out relatively well . . . hit a couple little chunks of ice . . . other than that we're sitting right here thanking the good Lord for all His mercies."

"OK. How many souls on board?"

"Two on board, and also thanking you, gentlemen."

"Well, we haven't found you yet, but we're looking."

"OK. . . . we've got a little portable strobe sitting out on the wing. The aircraft is orange and should be relatively easy to spot. We'll listen . . . what type of aircraft . . . *Electra* . . . understand?"

"Uh . . . Roger . . . it's a *Lockheed Electra* . . . four engines so you should hear us. We're presently quite high while we're looking for you, but as soon as we find you, we'll come down and see you."

"OK. . . . we're running quiet on the ELT [1] for the time being . . . I am going off for another five minutes unless I hear you . . . and I'll get back to you."

A few minutes later, the radio again comes to life.

"OK. . . . we checked and the last position we had from you from Cape Dyer was Zero Eight Five degrees true, and you were about sixty-five nautical miles from Cape Dyer," Alpha Zulu reported. "And we have a message for you that Sondestrom has dispatched a helicopter. There is a helicopter on the way and we will inform you of his estimated time of arrival as soon as we get it. Over."

---

1. ELT is short for "Emergency Locator Transmitter." It's a device that can be manually or automatically activated to transmit a distress signal to a satellite, enabling rescuers to home in on a particular position.

"OK, I appreciate that . . . now let me see . . . I've got a straight stretch of ice here about a thousand feet . . . relatively smooth . . . although that chopper coming wouldn't have any problem. We're on white ice."

"All right . . . do you have your strobe on and your ELT on?"

"Uh . . . the ELT is not operating at this time . . . do you want me to turn it on?"

"Yes, please."

"OK. . . .we'll go on with the ELT. . . do you pick up the ELT?

"Uh . . . negative at this time."

"I'm going to try and pull it out."

"We're northwest of you and will be heading back down again to see if we can pick you up. . . so we should be there in about a couple of minutes."

"OK. . . . and did you copy the ELT?"

"Negative."

"OK. . . . I'm going to turn it back on now. I have to turn it off when I am transmitting. Thank you. We haven't heard you yet."

"OK. . . . they said . . . according to Cape Dyer that . . . we should be pretty close to your last position . . . coming back up to you again. We see a pretty good open . . . uh . . . were you close to . . . say a bare piece . . . with no ice, with no snow on it . . . almost like an open lake?"

". . . that's affirmative."

"OK. . . . fine . . . we should be coming up to your position . . . pretty soon."

"OK. . . . we'll listen for you . . . and get back with you in five minutes."

Some moments later we see the aircraft wing lights and I reach once more for the microphone. "You're about three miles off of

our position now" I radioed. "We're picking up your wing light."

"All right we've got you now . . . we'll get your coordinates over to Cape Dyer . . . and that'll be OK. . . . for now."

With that last transmission, the radio went silent. And we waited.

CHAPTER 4
"07 Lima, We're Going to Make a Drop."

Our OAT gauge reads thirty-seven degrees below zero and dropping rapidly. I glance up at the engine situated above the fuselage. *Why the sudden loss of oil?* I wondered. Heavy black streaks cover the entire tail section as well as the fuselage below the propeller. The extreme cold, however, prevents even the strongest inclination to climb up and investigate. Our main and overwhelming concern is to insulate ourselves somehow from the freezerlike environment. We begin gathering all burnable materials we can find and with the waterproof matches I included in my survival kit we start a fire. Charts cease to exist as thousands of miles go up in smoke. I hesitate to think of burning my logbook, a large one filled with the adventures of some 30,000 miles of mercy missions in the Philippine Islands. I wanted it preserved but knew that with the increasing cold it too might have to burn.

Aubrey trudged back to the aircraft to see what else might be burnable. Finding a few remaining charts and a book on aviation, he quickly feeds the fast-fading flames.

What will we burn next? I kept asking myself. There was really

Finding more items for the fire.

nothing else to burn and the fire will soon be out.

As if reading my thoughts, Aubrey spoke up, "We'll burn the airplane when there's nothing else. . . ."

Suddenly a voice crackles from the cockpit. "Lake 1107 Lima—are you there?"

Trying to overcome my clumsiness from the cold, I force myself back into the aircraft. The transmission is repeated.

"07 Lima, 07 Lima . . . Alpha Zulu . . . Are you there?"

Gripping a nearly frozen microphone, I reply, "Go ahead . . . Alpha Zulu."

"OK. . . . just advise you that the helicopter from Sondestrom is on the way. We haven't got the ETA[1] for you yet, but he has to refuel once before he reaches you and if you can just hold on for a couple of minutes . . . we'll tell you his ETA and you can turn

---

1. Estimated Time of Arrival

your ELT on before he gets there."

"OK. Very good . . . we'll stand by this frequency. We're building a fire to keep warm."

Aubrey spoke up. "Tell them we need some blankets."

I again reach for the microphone. "Uh . . . Alpha Zulu . . . are you still there?"

"Go ahead."

". . . if anyone comes nearby, tell them to drop a couple blankets."

I turn back to the fire. The book on aviation and two wooden oars are feeding the last few dying embers from the burning charts. We attempt to fan the flames toward us but the only benefit seems to be from the exercise itself. An uncontrollable shiver has become a permanent part of me. Suddenly our miracle box again comes to life.

"07 Lima . . . we're going to make a drop. Are you still there?"

"Alpha Zulu . . . we're with you."

"OK. . . . leave that light back on. . . . we're going to come over you low and we've got a few nice blankets here that you can sort of camp on until the chopper gets there."

Aubrey takes the microphone. "I tell you . . . you all are mighty sweet. . . do you have any passengers aboard?"

"Uh . . . negative . . . this is an ice patrol airplane . . . just ice patrol people in it."

The *Electra* makes a couple passes and then a final one before disappearing to the west. I watch each approach through the lens of my movie camera, hoping the 8x zoom might enable me to spot the blankets as they drop. At the same time I wanted to record this wonderful gesture on the part of the captain. I look through the lens but see nothing.

"You mean you didn't see it either?" Aubrey exclaims.

Because of the whiteout effect, neither of us had seen where the precious cargo had landed. I radio back to the pilot and ask the approximate position of the drop. Somewhat apologetically he replied that the drop was prior to our position. At the altitude and speed necessary for his aircraft, it was difficult to make a very accurate drop.

Faced with the inevitable—a dying fire and increasing cold—I knew I had to find the blankets, particularly for Aubrey. He had not been as prepared for the unlikely event of severe weather conditions, or for that matter, camping out on an ice floe! I hesitate by the fire for a last bit of warmth, and then cautiously pressing down with my heavy hiking boots to confirm a solid surface, I begin to step my way across the ice floe.

Surely this is a part of the planet where few human beings have ever touched. A feeling of mutual understanding and kinship with the astronauts becomes instantaneous as I relive their experience on the surface of the moon. So this is what it was like, with realism that no television or camera could ever convey. *How could life possibly exist in such a hostile and threatening environment?* I wondered.

The distant roar of ice breaking up brings back the grim reminder that I have a job to do. Somewhere out in that white wilderness is the life-giving warmth of blankets and I must find them. My hiking habits prove a blessing at this moment as muscles tighten in response to my efforts to walk across the ice.

The bitter cold strikes cruelly at the exposed skin surface on my face, forcing tears to my eyes. The tears instantly freeze into little icicles and I try to wipe away the supercooled droplets. Shallow breaths help filter out the extreme cold as I cup a gloved hand over my face. Boardlike and stiffened with the cold, the glove seems less abrasive than the stinging ice crystals upon my skin.

Pushing on against the relentless and piercing wind, I recall a line of poetry from Shakespeare learned in English class—*Blow, blow, thou winter wind; Thou are not so unkind as man's ingratitude.* I never before questioned the wisdom of this verse. Now I was. How could any human being cause such pain as this biting and fiercely penetrating Arctic wind?

How much longer could I go . . . or dare to go? I soon realize that my short walk is taking on every aspect of a real struggle but I force myself on, ice crystals continuing to pelt against my face. An uneasy feeling comes over me as I begin to see the danger of my venture. The sounds of ice breaking up, the snow-covered crevices, the uneven and jagged surfaces, all jolt my system as I trudge on. I glance up from time to time hoping for some change in the wall-to-wall whiteness that might reflect the blankets. My entire system begins to shout out painful protests as my steps become more labored.

I must find those blankets, I reason to myself. *Our fire will not continue to burn much longer.* Knowing with the onset of darkness I will be forced to turn back, I try to quicken my pace.

Stumbling momentarily into a knee-deep snowdrift, my eyes suddenly catch the suggestion of a small shadow directly ahead. New courage courses through my veins as the dark spot reveals its identity . . . one solitary blue blanket! Shaking off the freezing snow, I hug the blanket to my face and pause for a moment. I look carefully in several directions hoping to catch sight of the other. The sounds of ice breaking up become more frequent than I care to think about and I finally give up any idea of looking further. The thought of being separated by shifting platforms of ice from the only other human being is a frightening one. I knew I had to start back immediately.

Retracing my footsteps, I glance up at the darkening skies and discover beauty I had not thought possible in such a lifeless environment. Scarcely visible, a few rays of light from a hidden sun are breaking through and bringing a lifelike appearance to the anemic Arctic surface. A healthy pink glow spreads its warmth across the skies. The glistening ice fields pick up the reflection, projecting its warmth upon my heart. Someone is in charge of things, even in this frozen, forgotten bit of our world. He who brought it into existence is still monitoring its course.

Returning to the fire, I hand the blanket to a very cold and grateful friend. The incessant cold seems to pervade every fiber of our beings and we both understand the potentially hazardous implications.

We soon learn that another aircraft, a *DC3,* has located our position. It will continue to circle our location until the helicopter's arrival and then will assist during the rescue operation. With little left of our dying fire and nothing more to burn, we comfort ourselves that the helicopter will soon be arriving.

Draining fuel for the fire as the DC3 circles

CHAPTER 5
"How Long Can You Survive?"

The arrival of the *DC3* is a most comforting sight as darkness settles upon us. It begins to circle our position, its engines droning out rhythmic reassurances of its presence. The momentary warmth of feeling created by a colorful Arctic twilight has vanished but the blinking lights of the aircraft above seem to carve a defensive line of protection around us. *My gratitude to the captain of that ship!*

With the daylight hours behind us, a night rescue would now be unavoidable. Night, an unenviable time for a pilot—when engines seem to run rougher and fuel burns hotter, when radios cut out and transponders turn temperamental, when mountains seem higher and runways shorter, and flight and life itself are dependent upon batteries and generators. Our rescue now will depend upon that small source of illumination.

The frequent communications with the *DC3* captain and the assurances of the soon arrival of the helicopter makes our dwindling fire less of a concern. As time passes, we begin thinking of the rescue operation. We reason that the search and rescue helicopter should have no trouble setting down if enough light were available. The final minutes drag on as we wait, the bitter, relentless cold only intensifying our anticipation.

Suddenly a voice crackles from the cockpit. "An ice storm has developed," the *DC3* captain explains. "The helicopter has been forced to return to Greenland."

It is a most distressing message for we are fully aware of the dangers that exist under icing conditions.

"Twice they have attempted to get through to you," the captain continued, "but dangerous, heavy icing has forced them to turn back. Any attempt of rescue is impossible for the present." The captain then added with a matter-of-fact sympathy in his voice. "The storm may continue for as long as five days or more. How long can you survive?"

The question stirred our strongest emotions. The will to live cuts through all barriers . . . ice floes, subzero temperatures, threats of ice breaking up . . . all are overshadowed by the human spirit's indomitable will to survive. We consider our emergency supplies. There is enough food for at least five days with the extra dried fruits and nuts I added to our rations the day before departure. Water should be no problem with the aid of a special desalting kit included in my survival gear. A greater life threatening emergency however is the freezerlike environment which some unfortunate downed pilots have tragically experienced . . . an unsuspecting anesthesia from the relentless cold benumbing the senses. Yes, we could use more blankets and some means to convert fuel in our aircraft into heat. Since our departure from Frobisher Bay we calculated we had consumed two hours of fuel from the auxiliary tank and a little less than an hour from the main tank. This leaves us with nearly sixty gallons to burn.

Sensing our need for extra warmth and protection from the cold, the captain of the *DC3* decides to drop his entire emergency pack. As the aircraft approaches and recognizing the difficulty of an accurate drop I take shelter under a wing. My concern however is short-lived. Cautiously peering out from under the wing I see the wing lights of the *DC3* momentarily suspended in space about thirty yards from our position. Suddenly the sound of surging engines and a brightly burning flame on the ice tells us the drop has been made. We immediately begin to step our way across endless chunks of ice to reach this precious cargo.

We assume the fire to be part of the procedure used to assist survivors in locating the drop. Upon examination, however, we discover that a kerosene stove dropped from the plane had broken apart from the impact, causing the flame. The drop included two sleeping bags, a tent, a rifle which had become dislodged into several pieces, fishing equipment, a pressure cooker with a broken handle, an ax, and wood tied in a bundle that appears to be the remains of an orange crate. We decide to take the sleeping bags first and struggle with the rest later. The urge to crawl into one for warmth has become an overpowering desire.

The extra thick sleeping bags feel like heavy bags of cement as we struggle to drag them over giant-size pieces of ice toward the plane. Trying to activate sore, stiffened fingers to untie the rope around a sleeping bag is equally exhausting. I return to the radio to transmit our appreciation for the supplies dropped.

Thinking of the rifle, I ask if there is any wildlife in the area. Earlier I had heard what sounded like Arctic terns flying overhead, the only other sound besides the frequent roar of moving ice breaking up.

The transmission immediately comes back. "Ma'am, that's the reason for the gun, because of the polar bears."

A new fear grips me. I had not yet thought about the possibility of polar bears. Now it all comes clearly to mind . . . the zoo

. . . those massive white bears with their incredible sense of smell reaching long distances. I had heard of their unusual swimming ability from ice floe to ice floe and now we are on an ice floe! Just the thought of a roaming polar bear revived my previous impulse to climb back into the aircraft. When expressed audibly, my idea is met with a strong communication . . . once and then again.

"Do not . . . we repeat. . . do not get back into the airplane."

The thought however continues to reinforce the desire.

As we watch the lights of the friendly *DC3* disappearing into the West, we decide to recover the remaining contents of the drop. We are alone now, two captive figures in the midst of a mass of frozen monuments, preparing to spend the night in the confines of the Arctic's cold storage. How long will we remain? We dare not estimate. With the help of our flashlights, we retrieve all that we are able to find including a box of powder I later discover to be red dye. I salvaged it only because the cardboard container would be burnable.

I take inventory of our meager supplies and place them under a wing of the aircraft. Daily rationing of food and water will be my responsibility and Aubrey will provide shelter by setting up the tents.

"I'll take apart the airplane if necessary," Aubrey emphatically says.

How I wish now for the protection of one of those igloos I had seen as we flew over Fort Chimo.

Finding the pressure cooker, Aubrey dislodges its cover with the ax. I then fill it with several quarts of fuel drained from the sump at the side of the aircraft. Tossing in a match we immediately have a brightly burning fire. It burns for about forty minutes and the same process is repeated throughout the night to keep the fire burning.

The dry, cold air seems to cause constant thirst. Finding a small cup I begin melting some of the ice but discover it to be salty. How thankful I am now for the desalting kit purchased for the emergency pack. Earlier we had yielded to the overwhelming urge to lick up some of the ice crystals forming on the wing of the airplane. As a nurse I knew better . . . the hazards of hypothermia and importance of retaining body heat. We never tried it again!

CHAPTER 6
A Night on a Moving Ice Floe

How does one prepare for a night in the Arctic? I wondered. I check our equipment: two sleeping bags, two tents, a rifle, water prepared from our desalting kit and a pot for fuel to keep the fire burning. Yes, and that Someone to keep us awake and alert through a night of life-threatening, freezing temperatures and hostile polar bear activity. We both knew our survival depended upon divine help.

Needing a comfort room in such an unfriendly environment proved to be most inconvenient. The thought of falling in the darkness through an unseen crevice of ice provided postponement of even the simplest habits. The need however finally forces me across the ice. *How much we take simple conveniences for granted,* I thought.

Returning to the fire, I unpack my tent. It's a small one purchased at Sears following a sixty-second demonstration by an enthusiastic salesman. He convinced me it was simple, quick, and easy to put up. How thankful I am for it now. What a relief this small shelter will be from the wind chill which is rapidly dropping temperatures even more. It is bitterly cold and I am anxious to set it up and crawl inside. I soon discover however that it's a major effort just to try and fit two aluminum pieces together. I struggle, fingers stiffened from the cold. Even without gloves it was an impossible task!

Succumbing to the cold, to the narcotic effect of the night, and the fact that Aubrey is already buried somewhere beneath a pile of tarpaulins, I lay down my tent. The howling winds seem to taunt my feeble efforts to steal a protected corner of their domain for myself. The enclosure of a sleeping bag will be my only shelter for the night. I spread it over the tent cover and begin crawling into bed . . . a bed of twelve inches of solid ice! Scraping off the snow from my boots, I lift them in first and then struggle to wiggle in the rest of a very bundled-up body. Even the roughest camping trip had not prepared me for such a challenge. My thickly padded jacket proves to be a lifesaver . . . one my husband

"It has to be the red jacket," said Bill.

insisted we purchase while at Sears looking for a small tent.

"It has to be the bright red one," Bill had said as he looked over the jackets. He then added, "It will make it easier to be seen when you go down on the ice." I was strongly objecting when the saleslady quickly wrapped the red one around my shoulders.

"You'll definitely be seen in this one," she confidently stated. Bill gave me a nod and I tried it on. It was surprisingly comfortable and large enough to fit over my other woolen jacket.

"Yes, it would actually be good to have an extra jacket," I admitted. Unknowingly, Bill had bought me the most important purchase of the day.

I finally struggle inside the sleeping bag, pulling a corner of it tightly around my head. It is cold . . . bitterly cold and I need every bit of warmth I can get. The pungent smell of tarp makes me wonder just what other unfortunate individual used this last for survival.

Ice crystals begin falling more rapidly as the winds increase. We sense the storm is fast approaching, the one which turned back the helicopter from a rescue attempt. The OAT (outside air temperature) has dropped to an unbelievable low. Adding to this is the threat of the wind chill factor creating the most frigid conditions for survival.

Keeping the sleeping bag tightly closed around my head lessens the cold, but I realize the serious effects of a lack of oxygen and undetected concentration of carbon dioxide. I am forced to open a peek hole for frequent whiffs of fresh air. This small opening soon becomes encrusted with ice. I know that to doze off with the sleeping bag either open or closed will prove life-threatening. The first would freeze fingers, toes and maybe more; the latter, perhaps slow suffocation in one's own breath. I am tired. I desperately want to sleep, but the continual opening and closing of the sleeping bag, though inconvenient, keeps me awake and becomes a life-saving maneuver. I wiggle my toes, flex my fingers, and roll from side to side. I know my survival depends on movement and staying awake. Exchanges of encouragement prove an added stimulus.

"How ya doin?" Aubrey would frequently drawl.

"Cold, very cold," became the usual response.

We take turns filling the pressure cooker with fuel drained from the sumps of the aircraft. A lighted match ignites the fuel which continues to burn for about forty minutes. When the fire is out, we drag the pan over and drain more fuel from the sump, repeating the process all over again. We are careful to move the pan each time as the thought of making contact with the icy waters of the Davis Strait even through a small hole is not a comforting one. The realization that the platform of ice we are on might be moving did not concern us as much as how thick it was. A step into oblivion is a terrifying thought as I watch the ice turning to liquid around the bottom of the pan. Our twelve inches of protection no longer exists in the areas where the pan has been.

The fire soon burns a hole through the side of the pan resulting in fingers of fire that reach out in every direction, fanned by the increasing winds. I vainly try to pull them toward me in an attempt to contain a little of the heat. It was a delicate maneuver to keep from getting burned and at the same time capture a little of the warmth.

Aubrey dragged his sleeping bag to a sheltered spot under the thirty-eight-foot wing span of the airplane. He had earlier pieced together the gun dropped from the plane, and now, perhaps in a confidence gaining maneuver, he places it by his head inside his sleeping bag. I later learned that the gun was not much comfort to him. It was merely an old .22/.410 combo—a 22-caliber rifle over a 410 gauge shotgun—one which would hardly phase a polar bear. Knowing little about guns, my main concern was whether Aubrey could reach for it quickly enough with his numbed fingers to take aim. I remember as a small child running in terror at the sight of my brother pointing Dad's old hockey stick at me. It was rigged with a clothespin holding a rubber band ready to fire. The painful stinging results of those "bull's eye" shots had left me with a strong dislike for weapons of any kind.

Somehow in sheer exhaustion I must have dozed off. For how long I do not know. Awakening in the darkness, I find myself fighting the confinement of what seems to be a strait jacket. Feeling for an opening, I strain my eyes to look out as a blast of cold air strikes my face. It seems as if I have opened the door to the North Pole. Suddenly the realization of where I am paralyzes me. It isn't a dream. I am actually here in nowhere, not even a spot on an aeronautical chart . . . just a couple of coordinates and what many would presume a probable statistic.

I notice the fire has gone out and there is not a sound from Aubrey. For one agonizing moment the thought that he had frozen to death terrifies me. *How did I ever let this happen?*

I realize that both of us had drifted off to sleep which we had hoped to prevent by often calling to each other. "Aubrey, are you alright?" I anxiously call out. There is no response. I call louder. Total silence.

Finally a startled voice emerges, "What is it?"

Oh, thank You, Lord, he's alive! I sigh in relief.

Sensing it was his turn to replenish the fuel, Aubrey responds, "I'm just too cold, Dorothy, just too cold!" I sense frustration in his usual matter-of-fact tone.

The thought of a hungry polar bear worries me more now that

the fire is no longer burning. Thinking the flames of the fire would be a deterrent to prowling bears, I felt a certain sense of security. Perhaps Aubrey was thinking similar thoughts, as I heard him begin to stir. He reaches out from his sleeping bag and tosses me a small cup to fill with fuel. "Fill it and I'll get the fire burning again," he says half-apologetically.

My struggle out of the half-frozen sleeping bag was as much of an effort as crawling in. It was simply too cold and too difficult. I decide to crawl still inside the bag dragging it with me over to the fuel sump, the same sump I had been using. Startled, I find it frozen—frozen solid. I decide to crawl over to the other side where there is another fuel sump but it will take too much effort to drag the sleeping bag with me. I will need to crawl out and face the bitter Arctic air.

It was a painful and difficult maneuver but finally emerging from the stiffened bag, I inch my way through the darkness to the other side of the aircraft. *Please, Lord, don't let this sump be frozen,* I pray. I reach out and touch the icy, cold sump. It is not frozen! It drains . . . precious life giving fuel. *Oh thank you, Lord.*

Soon a fire is burning again and we continue through the night to drain fuel from the same sump. Never once did that particular sump ever freeze during our long Arctic night. Angels must have spread their wings over that sump, I thought to myself.

I cannot bear to think of crawling back into my sleeping bag. It is damp and half frozen. Aubrey feels the same way and we hover close to the flames, turning our backs and then our faces to absorb a little of the heat. We begin to discuss plans for what might well be a five-day ordeal, or perhaps even longer should the ice storm continue. The thought of even one more night on the ice is painful enough in our struggle to survive. An ice-stiffened sleeping bag will need to be thawed out and dried. I know only too well this might never happen with the approach of the coming storm.

CHAPTER 7
Thoughts on Trial

The fire seems to have a hypnotic effect upon my mind as I continue to stare at the flickering flames. Again the thought returns, *is this really happening to me?* I remember as a child dreaming about the North Pole, wondering what it would be like to live in that mysterious place. The winter winds whistling around the buildings and through the trees of our Montana farm reinforced the realism of it all. And now I was experiencing that dream.

Thoughts tumble one upon another as I reflect upon the warm tropical islands of the Philippines. There I had spent the last year in medical flights with our 1964 *Piper Aztec* that I had flown across the Pacific. Many isolated islands without airstrips still wait, reachable only by slow Banka boat. The idea of a seaplane was born shortly after a thirteen-year-old girl was brought by arduous boat trip too late to our plane. She died just moments after arrival. The tragedy of this young girl haunted me and I was determined to return home to California for an amphibious aircraft. An aircraft which could reach isolated islands without airstrips, where patients could be transported easily and quickly for medical care.

My thoughts turn to those waiting. There is Manuel, whom I promised to transport for much needed surgery. Four-year old Maria, unable to walk, with congenital heart disease is also in need of an operation. Venida knows I'm returning for I promised.

Suddenly my thoughts are interrupted as the last bit of fuel for the fire is being consumed. I realize it's my turn to refuel . . . more fuel for more dreams . . . dreams yet to be accomplished, or perhaps lost and forever buried in the Arctic.

Somehow a small spark of reassurance burns through the seemingly impenetrable cold exterior and touches a heart yet filled with hope. Rescue and fulfillment will come. *A familiar verse comes to mind, it comes from my own experience here on the ice . . . yes, my valley is an ice floe, the shadow of death, the Arctic's cold grip. "Though I land on an ice floe in the Arctic, I will fear no evil: for Thou art with me." He's promised, "Whatsoever ye ask in my name, believing, ye shall receive"* (Matthew 21:22). Yes, I wanted much for the islands, a mission plane to fly again for those promised . . . Manuel, Maria, Venida, and many others. *But how now, Lord?*

In a cold and eerie silence I continue my thoughts, interrupted only by the occasional thunderlike sounds of more ice breaking up. How was it all to end? A seaplane buried in the frigid waters of the Arctic? A final flight plan closed? For how long I was trapped in this filmstrip of fate, I do not know, but as darkness—real and forever—closed in around me, I began to reflect on my life and how it all began.

The year was 1929. The Great Depression had engulfed every household across America and our family was no exception. I was born during those difficult times, very much wanted, but hardly afforded. My father was a pastor and already the budget was being stretched to the limit. With four in the family now to support, it was becoming a matter of survival.

My father tells about one experience when I was just a few months old that reveals the desperate situation in which so many were suffering. It was a day when my father and mother needed a few supplies at the grocery store. Father parked their Model T Ford near the store and they hurried inside while I was sleeping in the back seat.

It was but a short time later that they walked out of the store to the car. To their shock and disbelief they discovered their car jacked up with all four wheels missing. Still in the back seat in a basket however was their little baby girl sleeping soundly. To kidnap a baby would only mean another mouth to feed. Wheels were far more valuable!

Mother taught violin lessons to supplement the meager income and Father kept a garden which supplied much of our food. My father, as a pastor-evangelist, spent long hours traveling throughout the states of Iowa, and later Montana. These were happy times for me as he often took family along with him. I grew up listening to many of my father's sermons. He had a portable building called "The Silver Temple" for his evangelistic meetings which he moved from place to place. I remember the chairs were painted silver, also the songbooks and the pulpit . . . all were painted silver. Someone suggested that Mother's violin she played each evening should also be painted silver. Mother did not look kindly at the idea and her bow took priority over the brush! Even when I was young, my father's sermons seemed to have a strong influence on me. He tells of an evening meeting when he spoke on the state of the dead, citing Scriptures that compare death to sleep. Returning home that evening, he was unable to get me to sleep. He told story after story and gave many hugs but nothing seemed to work. Finally exasperated, he held me close and whispered, "Dottie dear, please tell daddy why you can't go to sleep."

General Conference globe

"I'm afraid if I go to sleep I might wake up and find myself dead," I answered with tears in my eyes. My father felt he must have preached a most powerful sermon that night!

I admired my father greatly and decided at a young age I wanted to be just like him, a minister. In those days, the thought of a woman becoming a minister was inconceivable. "Women can be Bible Workers," Father told me, recognizing my disappointment. Growing older, I decided that if I could not *be* a minister, I would *marry* one.

My childhood was a happy one and I relived again the closeness I had with family. I remember a very special attraction in our home, a large globe sitting on my father's desk. The moments I shared with him turning the globe and finding all the little islands in the big oceans excited me. I wondered if there were missionaries that lived on any of these islands. My aunt and uncle were missionaries in India and I was always thrilled whenever I found a letter in the mailbox with a certain foreign stamp on it. I just knew there would be pictures and stories that Mother would share. How I wanted to be a missionary! My father assured me that God did have a special place for me somewhere on that globe. And I believed him.

"Just pray about it, Dottie, for if God wants you there, you'll be there."

Another globe capti-

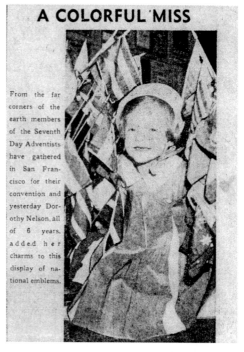

A COLORFUL MISS

From the far corners of the earth members of the Seventh Day Adventists have gathered in San Francisco for their convention and yesterday Dorothy Nelson, all of 6 years, added her charms to this display of national emblems.

Six years old at the General Conference in San Fransisco

vated my interest about this same time. I was six years old when I first saw this special globe. My father was attending a General Conference session in San Francisco and had brought along the family. In the convention center where the meetings were being held was a very large and unique globe with lights around it that twinkled. The globe became a favorite meeting place for our family.

"I'll meet you at the globe" my father would often say. I would always plan to be at the globe early and wait, totally captivated by the lights. Other families and friends used the globe as a meeting place but to me it became more than a meeting place. . . . It was part of a dream that would carry me someday to one of those lights. Every opportunity I had would find me standing and watching the lights. It was another General Conference session later that I stood at that same globe watching the many more lights that had been added. It was thrilling to see them all and I picked out the place where someday I would be a missionary. My father had said it and I believed him.

"God does have a place for you somewhere on that globe."

When I was eight years old, Amelia Earhart was making head-lines flying an airplane around the world. It became the topic of conversation in many homes and ours was no exception. As the news followed this woman pilot around the globe, so did my thoughts. Perhaps an airplane could reach the faraway islands on my father's globe. I would learn to fly! I will find those wings that will carry me to one of those distant islands.

I first tried those wings unsuccessfully at the age of nine. It was a child's day to dream. Cotton candy clouds floated tantalizingly overhead as I watched them drift where I could not follow. Some-day I would follow, but now I could only listen as they spoke to me. They told me of following rivers which never seem to end, of tall pines which reach through their misty borders, of meadows that drink from their overflowing reservoirs, and of children who see through their frosted windows . . . finding elephant heads, ti-ger tails, and friendly faces. At times they become castles wearing caps like mushrooms, thin ribbons that stretch and break in two, and dark shadows . . . gray and ghostlike . . . that thunder and shout. They bring a premature night to an overactive child who is forced to find shelter as tiny brown puddles become rushing rivers submerging little feet. I wondered why those dark ones shouted at each other and then suddenly disappeared, leaving an empty blue playground. I watched for them and they always returned, some-times as only dots and dashes, in a hurry to leave again.

This day in June they seemed to be little cotton balls all in a row, as if spectators about to witness an unfolding drama. Gentle

My first attempt to fly!

My brother . . . my hero!

afternoon breezes prompted my eleven year old brother, Rich, to try out the special secret I had shared with him. We talked about it on the ball field, in the limbs of the old cherry tree, and on our hikes down to the pond. I had practiced jumping through the air off a sandy cliff and just knew that I could learn to fly. Rich said it, and I believed it. The day had finally come and I was to have my first flying lesson. Rich would be the control tower to clear me for my very first takeoff.

It was a day when my father and mother were away preparing for a camp meeting that my brother announced, "This is a perfect day for your first flying lesson with a 'just right' breeze."

I was thrilled! The sky . . . the clouds . . . all were beckoning me. *Yes, this is the day! I am going to fly!* My bedroom was on the second floor of our rented farmhouse and Rich joyfully said that my window sill was the perfect place to take off on my first flight. He was very excited about it and said he could just see a spectacular takeoff. I myself could hardly wait as Rich gathered up mother's plush pillows and soft woolen blankets placing them on the grass below my bedroom window. He then brought me father's big black umbrella as I squatted on the window sill.

"I'll tell you when to jump," Rich said. "Just hold on tightly to the umbrella and it will carry you gently down to the landing area below."

My dream was coming true and I wanted to make this first flight the very best ever. I soon heard Rich shouting, "Cleared for takeoff." Holding on tightly to the handle of the umbrella I looked down and saw Rich waving me on.

"Jump, Dot, jump!" he shouted.

With all my might I jumped out as far as I could. I was in the air. I was flying! My dreams were coming true. Suddenly . . . I was not flying. I was falling and very fast with a collapsed umbrella. Just as suddenly I hit bottom with a very hard landing in spite of the pillows and blankets. My ankles hurt and I cried out in pain. Worse yet my first flight had been a complete failure. Rich tried to comfort me and said something about the winds. It was not long when Father and Mother returned and discovered our secret. My ankles were wrapped, and Rich learned more about how things fly!

As I grew older Mother shared with me the miracle of her life and why music has been such a part of her. She was brought up in a musical family and often on the stage in concert with her sisters, "The Kipp String Quartet," as they were known. They were tutored in the summer and gave concerts during the school year. When Mother was still in her teens, the quartet performed at the Hutchinson Theological Seminary[1] where my father, Joseph Nelson, attended school. Father saw her picture in the

---

1. Hutchinson Theological Seminary, also called Maplewood Academy, was a regular college during this time.

program and picked her out as the young woman he was going to marry someday.

One summer, a colporteur visited the Kipp family where they lived on Lake Pulaski in Minnesota. My grandmother, a deeply religious person, bought one of the books, *The Desire of Ages*. She was invited to attend a series of Seventh-day Adventist evangelistic meetings and was convinced of the Sabbath truth. My grandmother was soon baptized as was my mother, at sixteen, who also attended the meetings.

The quartet was separated when Mother set aside her violin for a bicycle to canvass, selling religious books, in her town for the summer. Her sister Maude joined her, and the two girls earned enough money to attend college the following year. Their older sister, Winnie, married and went to Serbia as an ambassador's wife. Maude married a minister, Olaf Skau, and sailed for India where they remained the rest of their active lives, the missionaries who so inspired me.

My mother returned to Hutchinson Theological Seminary to take the Normal Course as well as to teach violin. There she met my father, still studying to be a minister. He was able to win her heart . . . the same girl he had picked out in the program notes of the Kipp String Quarter concert the year before. How much I have to be thankful for! My father and mother have influenced, inspired, and motivated me to do something with my life for God. And this has been my dream.

It was at college that I met another Nelson . . . his name was Wilbur, but to most he was simply Bill. He had just returned from Norway where he had been an exchange student. Hearing of my Norwegian heritage, Bill enjoyed sharing his experiences which he had while a student in Oslo. As we became better acquainted, we shared our ideas of being missionaries to some foreign country.

Bill was studying Spanish and talked about his interest in South America. His uncle was fluent in Spanish and had been a missionary to that area of the world field.

I soon discovered that Bill was a pilot but that didn't spoil our friendship. Noticing my sensitivity, he quickly learned to avoid the subject. As our friendship grew stronger during the next year I could see that Bill desired an even closer relationship. I felt there was something however I should explain to him. "You're a very special friend, Bill, but I do need to share something that is very important to me. When I become serious about getting married, it will be to a minister. This has been my dream since a little girl and I do hope you understand."

I thought our friendship would surely end at this point for I knew his father, a physician, wanted him to take the medical course. I felt sad about losing his friendship, but my dream to marry a minister was an all-consuming passion. I craved the relationship my father and mother had in working together in ministry. I prayed earnestly about it and felt the Lord would lead me to the right companion. It was only a short time later that I learned Bill had changed his course to theology . . . he had decided to study for the ministry! He did not tell me for some time, but this caused even a deeper attraction for this missionary-minded friend. It became more and more evident the Lord was leading us into a deeper relationship.

With the school year finished I would return home to Glendale where family had moved due to my father's work with the Pacific Union Conference. Before going our separate ways for the summer, Bill invited me to spend an afternoon with him. He would be canvassing during the summer and this would be our last time together for some months. I cherished our visits together as Bill always came up with new ideas of missionary work. This day it seemed the Lord was calling our attention to something beyond the place . . . to the actual missionaries themselves. Yes, in the back of my mind I realized that God was drawing us closer to being a missionary team. I knew He would then direct us where this missionary team should go.

Driving into the countryside that afternoon, Bill passed by a small airport. He paused for a moment and pointed out a little airplane which he said his brother owned. He called it a *J3 Cub,* which didn't mean much to me as I didn't know one airplane from another. Looking seriously over at the airplane, Bill suddenly put his arm around me and pleaded, "Just a short flight . . . just one, please."

I was so surprised that I couldn't say anything for a moment. He had never talked about flying and seemed to respect and understand whatever feelings I had. Now I must explain to him that there was a time I really wanted to fly . . . and it actually had much to do with missions. I wanted him also to know I wasn't questioning his flying ability but that my first flight with an umbrella had been a complete failure and frightened me terribly.

"Why, Dottie, there is a world of difference between an umbrella and an airplane," he said in a rather jovial but sympathetic tone. Then he added, "It will only be a short flight, I promise, and one of my very best!"

He was absolutely sure I would enjoy every minute of it once I was in the air. I'll never forget the feeling of wrapping a belt around me in that little airplane. I felt trapped with no way out but I must do this for the one who had become a very special part of my life. I repeated again his promise, "It will only be a short one."

Bill knew that I enjoyed acrobatics when I was growing up and decided he would demonstrate a maneuver called a loop. He was confident I would just love it. He explained it in detail and I thought to myself, *Anything to get this flight over with and back on the ground.* We were soon up in the air and I began to feel this wasn't so frightening after all. In fact, I was beginning to enjoy looking out the window. The skies were a brilliant blue and the countryside ablaze with color. It was springtime. I had never imagined how incredibly beautiful things would appear from the air and really how delightful flying could be.

"Dottie, isn't it wonderful? See how easy the little plane flies?" I felt proud of Bill who was doing his best to make it a special and happy flying experience for me. As the airplane climbed higher and higher into the sky, childhood dreams sharpened into focus. I seemed to be in a swing again . . . my little feet stretching upward to touch the clouds. *But it's for real this time. I am flying!*

Bill soon started into the loop and then repeated it . . . up and over again and again. I began not only to tolerate these aerobatics but actually to enjoy them. On one of the loops however he did something which he had not explained. As later described he "kicked left rudder, pulled back on the stick" and we were suddenly in a spin heading straight towards the ground! Comfortable feelings immediately vanished and I was convinced I had made a terrible mistake after all. *Why did I ever try flying again?* I cried to myself.

I was sure we were going to crash into the ground when Bill suddenly shouted, "There's something I've been wanting to ask you. Ah . . . ah . . . Dottie, ah . . . will you marry me?" I was shocked, dazed, yet charmed all at the same time! Trying to overcome my complete surprise as well as regain my composure I shouted back, "Yes, anything . . . just get this plane back safely on the ground!"

A flashback of my earlier experience with a very hard landing panicked me. Seemingly at ease, Bill brought the little plane out of the spin and made a very soft landing. Yes, literally "engaged in a spin!" Once on the ground there was a big hug for the pilot from a very excited passenger. The spin did put a bride in his arms but it came with a price. "Please don't ask me to fly again . . . it's just too frightening!"

Out of love and respect for this very special person, the young pilot put away his license. There it remained in a box of memories hidden from view until a quarter of a century later when those wings were unfolded again encouraged by the same bride who had said she never wanted to fly again.

The sheer delight of that moment—that day—and the feelings expressed were discovered on handwritten hotel stationary incredibly by the same girl who had said "yes" when asked to marry this young pilot now turned pastor. She shares now the words he wrote—with fond memories and a few smiles!

"Folded wings . . . 1948–1974"

My flying years were 1945–47, age 16–18, with the private ticket issued three days after my 17th birthday. Those were adventuresome days and then I met Dottie in the first year of college at 18. By the end of the year, I knew that love for her was real and even more than my love for flying. Yet I wanted both and was sure that Dottie would love flying too. She didn't. Why she wasn't thrilled I don't know but I had noticed some others who didn't care for my flying either like that *Constellation* pilot who had to get out of my way when I was practicing stalls in his flight path over San Fernando Valley! But somehow I must help Dottie learn to love flying. If she

"Engaged in a spin"

only felt the thrill of flying I'm sure she would just fall in love with it. I thought that maybe her folks are against it. I decided to take her mother for a ride first and then her dad. It was a perfect day for flying with very little breeze. I flew the pattern with mother while Dottie and her dad waited at the side of the little airstrip. Busy putting mother at ease, my approach to the little field was a bit high. I did a rather violent slip over the end of the airstrip coming quite close to the trees (with one wing pointing to the ground). Mother closed her eyes and gasped. Later I learned that Dottie's dad turned pale and looked away while Dottie stood speechless. Dad did finally manage a weak smile but declined a ride saying, "It's getting a bit late."

We were married by my father on August 21, 1949. It was a very special and thrilling moment to walk down the aisle with Father by my side and to repeat our vows with him as the minister! The wedding was followed by several years of pastoral and evangelistic activities. Then it was ordination and a call to serve in the mission field. A childhood dream was being fulfilled. Those distant islands on my father's globe were coming into focus and I would soon have the opportunity to share this love with a minister husband. How incredible is God's plan for His children!

"We'll let you have your baby first!"

The gentleman spoke with a bit of humor as I was experiencing another strong contraction in the labor room. *How did he get in here anyway?* I wondered.

I was shortly to be wheeled into delivery when the nurses discovered this friendly gentleman was not my brother or even a family member. He was Brother Norman Dunn in charge of mission appointees for the South American Division. Bill knew Spanish well and the call was to Aruba. The reason this good "brother" had to see me so urgently was that he needed an immediate answer to start processing the mission call. Bill had agreed to accept the call while visiting with him in the waiting room. Brother Dunn had been a former Bible teacher of mine and Bill felt confident that I would surely love to see him with such an exciting request. After all, this had been our dream for the past several years.

"Just step into the labor room . . . she'll be happy to see you and will agree immediately!" my husband happily assured him.

However, as Brother Dunn was beginning to talk to me about the call, I was quickly whisked to the delivery room. The baby— our first—was transverse and the delivery turned out to be a very difficult one. Additional time would be needed for my recovery and consequently we were unable to accept the call. Several years later, however, another invitation came while Bill was youth pastor of the Loma Linda Campus Hill church. This time the call was to the island of Formosa. We knew nothing about the Chinese language and had hardly even heard of the island. Additionally, Bill was receiving pressure to stay as youth pastor with the Campus Hill Church.

"Let others go . . . your particular talents are needed here . . . the mission field of Loma Linda!" was often repeated.

There were challenges on every side to deter us from accepting this call. "Anyone can go over there and do that work . . . your children are so young . . . it's too dangerous . . . every call isn't always from the Lord . . . leaders do make mistakes in judgment!"

and the list went on.

Well-meaning and sincere friends pointed out what they felt were good reasons to turn down this call. "Not everyone can relate to the youth as you are doing here in Loma Linda." It was a difficult decision but we turned to our favorite author for her encouragement and counsel.

We studied. We prayed earnestly and relied on His Word. We were confident it was God's will that we accept the call. "Come over to Macedonia (Formosa) and help us," kept ringing in our ears. My father was with the General Conference at this time and we valued his counsel very much. He had seen other mission appointees leaving families for overseas appointments. He knew the feelings . . . what it meant . . . the long absence from children and grandchildren. Now it was his family. Yes, he and mother would miss us terribly, especially the little grandchildren. They knew the struggle all parents have as their families become separated for long periods.

"Go and follow the Lord's leading. He never makes a mistake," was my father's counsel.

He was proud of our decision and I will never forget the day we sailed out of the San Francisco harbor. My father and mother with my younger brother, Deane, stood at the dock holding their end of the long yellow streamer as the *Indian Bear* pulled away from the shore. We waved; we cried; we threw kisses as we continued to hold on to the streamer. It soon pulled tighter and tighter and finally snapped. It seemed like a final goodbye as we watched the streamer twist and turn and then settle on the choppy waters. Family became mere specks on the horizon and I thought to myself, *Theirs is the sacrifice not ours! Oh, heavenly Father, please take care of them until we meet again.*

As the ship passed under the Golden Gate Bridge, I was re-

Saying goodbye to family as we board the Indian Bear

minded again how God answers even the simplest prayer . . . the prayer of a little nine-year-old girl wanting to reach some distant island for Jesus. Yes, and with a minister husband and a bonus of two precious children. How much better could it be?

———————

"It's all up to father Neptune now!"

The sea captain muttered as he closed down the port holes of the old freighter we were on, *Indian Bear.* He then added, "Every time I take missionaries on board it turns out to be a rough trip and by the current weather report, you no doubt will be the best of that crowd!"

It was a very severe storm in which it was necessary to tie our two children in bed and brace ourselves in such a way as to avoid being thrown out. The morning hadn't started out well at the dining hall as a strong wave had tossed me into the captain's lap spilling his coffee. His only remark was "It's all up to father Neptune now, so no need to pray."

I watched the bow of the ship dig deeply into the churning seas and then lumbering, rise up again, then down again and back up again. The captain told us about an instrument that indicates at what point the ship could roll over. That night I decided to look for it. *Could this storm possibly be that violent?* I wondered. Bracing myself, I crawled up the stairway and found the instrument (something I learned later was an onboard inclinometer.) I discovered that the needle was right at the rollover point the captain had mentioned. *Please, Lord, don't let the needle go past that point,* I prayed.

We continued to pray throughout the night as we were tossed up and down. The ship creaked and groaned as if about to split apart. Each time the ship went down it seemed it might never come back up again. Doors were banging and water from a commode next to our bed splashed over with each wave. Down and back up . . . down and back up again. The swells seemed monstrous. *When will it ever end,* we wondered. We knew it was a very serious storm but we also knew we had another Captain who was in charge and we put our trust in Him.

Later as the storm finally subsided the captain told us it was the worst storm in all of his years of crossing the Pacific. Then he added, "It's just a good thing you missionaries were praying."

The captain was amazed at how many relatives we missionaries seemed to have at each port. It was "brother here" and "sister there" throughout the trip. He was most pleased to receive homemade cookies from our "sisters" at many of our stops. He later discovered that all these "sisters" and "brothers" were part of a worldwide church family.

CHAPTER 8
I Learn to Fly

"Mom, would you like to go out with me to the airport to watch Ken take his first flying lesson?" My daughter's words startle me. *Oh no, I thought, surely Ken's not taking up flying! I can just see Janet someday without a husband. Somehow I've got to try and dissuade him.*

I had definitely decided that flying was not safe with what I had experienced as a child and later as a soon-to-be-bride. The risks were simply too great. The family already knew that I had driven all night to avoid flying in a little airplane. Dr. Brueske, a long time friend and pilot offered to fly our family from the airport at Pacific Union College for an appointment scheduled the next morning at Loma Linda University. The family flew; I drove. All night long I traveled the long miles to avoid getting into that little airplane. Such was my fear of flying. It didn't help to watch the plane take off and narrowly miss the tops of the pine trees . . . or so it seemed.

I try to be as pleasant as possible as I ride with Janet out to the Collegedale Airpark. After all, I had not seen family for several years and furlough was always a special time. My husband who had projects to finish in the Philippines would be joining us a short time later. Arriving at the airport, we soon see Ken with his instructor walking around a small airplane. Janet explains to me they are doing what is called a preflight to make sure the plane is working properly. *She must think this will prevent anything from happening to the plane,* I thought to myself. I quickly decide on a plan so as not to hurt Janet's feelings or embarrass Ken. When the lesson is finished I will congratulate Ken and then have a little talk with the instructor to voice my concerns. In a nice way I will attempt to explain my feelings toward flying.

Ken's lesson being completed, Janet and I walk over to the airplane where Ken and his instructor are standing. Ken introduces me to the instructor who seems rather unassuming—not exactly what I thought a flight instructor would be like. I wasn't sure at that point just what to say.

"You know there's something that bothers me about flying. If you're in a car and your engine stops you're at least on the ground but in an airplane if your engine fails you don't seem to have much choice but to crash."

There was a noticeable pause as the instructor looked at me in a rather quizzical way. This bothered me and not knowing what to say next I added, "I really don't know that much about airplanes. Perhaps I need to know more . . . do you think you could educate me in a lesson or two?" I thought if I took a few lessons it would help me explain to Ken why I feel so strongly about his taking flying lessons and the risks involved. I then asked rather quietly, "you ever taught someone like me . . . like my age to fly?" I was sure he would have a dozen reasons why it wouldn't be possible. He might, however, at least take me up just once to answer some of my questions.

His answer was a complete surprise and stirred something deep within me. "Well . . . I just don't know why not!" he replied in his southern drawl. The next day found me at the airport taking what I thought was my first and only flying lesson. It was an unusually clear day as Janet drove me out to the Collegedale Airpark. There were little airplanes all tied down in a row including the red one that Ken had been flying with his instructor. The instructor selected this same one . . . what he called a *Cessna 150*. Names and numbers meant nothing to me at this point but I was happy it was the same plane that had come back safely with Ken. Soon we were walking around the airplane together as he talked and touched every part of it or so it seemed. Parts he called ailerons, parts he called flaps, and parts he called cotter pins. Every movable and immovable part. Through all this, however, the burning question in my mind kept haunting me, *What happens when the engine quits? Can flying ever be safe? This is all I really want to know.* I did wonder about checking the radiator when the instructor pulled out the dip stick to check the oil. I was too embarrassed to ask as I was already feeling quite apart from it all.

With the preflight inspection completed, the instructor orients me to the cockpit and taxis to the runway. He explains the different instruments on the panel and what to expect as the plane lifts off the ground. Stopping at the end of the taxiway, the instructor suddenly turns to me and says, "Now you take off."

He surely can't be serious, I thought. His nonchalant manner seemed to hide the fact that he definitely was planning for me to fly the airplane. *How did I get myself into this?* I begin to wonder, as I shortly find myself being talked through my first takeoff. Pushing in the power and building up speed I marvel at the ease with which the little plane starts to leave the ground. It literally seems to jump into the air . . . up into the sky.

We are flying! Soon the instructor takes the controls and flies what he calls "straight and level." He demonstrates how the rudder works, how the airplane turns, and how it climbs and descends. Suddenly as if reading my mind, *what if?* he pulls back on the throttle and something he calls carburetor heat. The plane becomes uncomfortably quiet and soon we are heading downward.

"Oh no, not this again," I tell myself. Memories of my flight with Bill race across my mind as the plane continues toward earth. The umbrella, the spin, and now this, all unravel the truth . . . flying is not safe!

The instructor very calmly explains the plane is able to glide and land safely. As the plane continues to come closer to the ground I could not believe what I was seeing. It was gliding not falling! So an airplane doesn't fall out of the sky after all, I reason to myself. Somewhere deep in my soul I begin to wonder . . . *Could this be the dream I thought was forever buried?* The imagined risk factor had suddenly become the launching pad for my desire to fly. That small spark, kindled in childhood was still there. Yes, I will learn to fly! I will find those wings. They are somewhere waiting. It's for me but to find them, fly them, and ultimately find fulfillment in them . . . in a remote village, a forgotten barrio, a distant island. And I continued to dream.

Weeks pass . . . and more lessons. I was beginning to enjoy the basic maneuvers of takeoffs, straight and level flight, turns, and the many, many landings. One day my instructor talks about the day I will solo.

"When it is safe enough to put my little boy in the plane with you, you will be ready to solo," the instructor explains.

I wanted the time prolonged however before the instructor stepped out of the plane. Somehow I had the impression that when he does I will be alone for a very long time. Alone in an airplane. Alone in the skies! I wasn't quite sure I was ready for this.

I Learn to Fly

Each day, I hoped it would be the next. I wanted as much flying experience as possible with the instructor. That "next day" did come as I was practicing take offs and landings in the pattern. The instructor suddenly opens the door of the plane and steps out. I stare at him as he walks away but he looks the other direction and motions me on. So this is it . . . the day I solo! There is no time to object and I taxi out toward the runway. *Am I really prepared for this?* I ask myself. I radio my intentions and push in the throttle. I take off . . . alone! The plane literally jumps into the air without the presence of my well-nourished instructor. He had informed me about this and how right he was! The plane quickly climbs up to the altitude of the pattern. I begin to wonder, *how will I ever get this plane back on the ground?* It seems to want to keep climbing . . . to soar . . . as I fly around the pattern.

My daughter and her husband had been forewarned from the instructor that I was more than ready to solo. They in turn prepared for what could be my solo day. Bill had arrived late the night before from the Philippines and wondered where I was going so early in the morning. I explained there was a sick lady I promised to see. She was actually the instructor's wife who had taken ill. Bill knew nothing at all about my flying which had been kept a very tight secret.

Later that morning Bill was invited to the airpark with Ken and Janet. They drove to the far side to watch any airplanes that might be flying in the pattern. Suddenly both Ken and Janet jump out of the car, grab their cameras and begin taking pictures of a little red *Cessna* coming in for a landing. Bill began thinking, *Wow! Ken really does have it bad . . . can't get flying out of his system.* Ken and Janet run around the car excitedly shouting, "C'mon dad, watch this airplane land!" The plane was just touching down. Not to dampen their excitement, Bill looked out the window toward the airplane.

"Well that was quite a nice landing," Bill remarked as the plane touched down. "Now why don't we find out where Mother is and head back home. It's been a long trip for me and I'm still on jet lag."

Ken and Janet quickly scramble into the car and drive over to the airpark office on the other side of the runway. They arrive just as the *Cessna* taxies up near the front entrance. I could see my instructor standing there with the broadest grin on his face. Bill stepped out of the car as I jumped out of the airplane. Just then everything broke loose!

"Where's the pilot?" Bill asks, astonished to see me anywhere near an airplane.

I rush over to Bill, throw my arms around him with a big bear hug and whisper, "I'm that pilot, Honey, . . . I just soloed." He was speechless. At that moment a large cake decorated with a little plane landing on a runway with the words, *"I did it!"* was presented to the last person Bill would ever have thought landed that airplane. He literally had to disappear into the office where he found a couch and collapsed . . . it was to him the shock and surprise of a lifetime!

As he sat dazed and in wonderment he began to mull over events of the past twelve hours. The call he made enroute home when Dottie asked him what latitude he was at didn't make sense and neither did Dottie's sudden departure early the next morning to see a sick lady. Ken's preoccupation with learning to fly was not characteristic of him and he thought *maybe I have been away too long.* However the joy of the moment, the excitement around him brought things into clearer focus as family and friends congratulated Dottie, the girl he thought he knew . . . afraid to fly!

Thus was the beginning of a dream that culminated in the licensing and ratings which I felt were necessary to become a safe missionary pilot. Subsequently I instructed in the twin and flew medical flights for physicians from the Loma Linda University Medical Center.

EXCERPT FROM PAUL HARVEY NEWS ...

JANUARY 23, 1975

How about Dorothy Nelson ...

Oakland, California nurse who was afraid to

fly ...

But she overcame her fear of flying by learning,

at 46, to pilot a plane herself ...

Today -- she flew across the Pacific.

With a friend she flew a twin engine Aztec across

the Pacific Ocean.

California to Manila!

"My supportive family were the 'power behind the props' . . . ever encouraging, ever attentive to patients and pilot alike! How could I have done without them?"

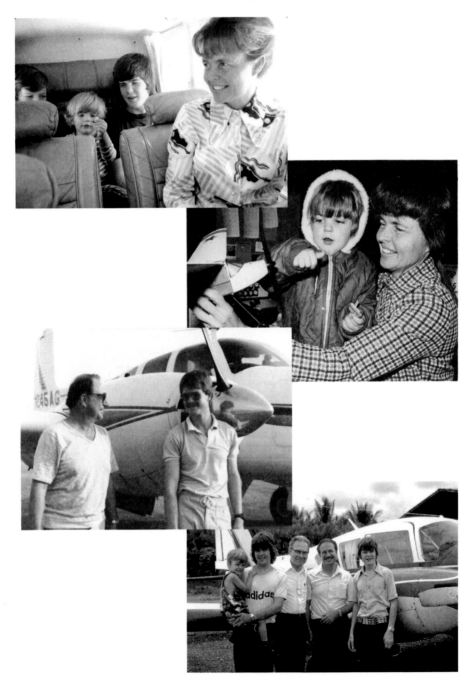

*"Family team departs for Malaysia to join
LaVerne and Alma Tucker in a Health Expo."*

CHAPTER 9
Arrival in Manila

"November 5500 Yankee, you're cleared to land."

The voice sounded more personal than the usual transmission for an airplane's arrival. It was more than words. It was the fulfillment of a dream . . . the answer to a little girl's prayer . . . a spot on a globe come alive! Yes, the words are heavenly music to one who believes that dreams do come true. Inspired by a father, encouraged by a husband, motivated by a brother and challenged by the needs of a distant country I was now landing our "much dreamed about," "much prayed about" airplane, a twin engine *Piper Aztec,* N5500Y.

As I touched down on the runway at the Manila International Airport, my heart was filled with praise to my heavenly Father for making this all possible. We did not know earlier where we would be able to find an airplane or even be able to purchase one as we had little funds. We prayed about it earnestly. One day my husband had the opportunity to speak with a friend, Ellsworth McKee, about our mission flying plans.

"The McKee Baking Company is retiring a twin-engine *Piper Aztec* from service," Ellsworth mentioned. "The company is in need of a larger aircraft."

A dream fulfilled

Although we did not have funds to purchase an airplane, we did own some property. We were thankful the board agreed to accept our property in lieu of payment for the aircraft.

With documents in order, I then flew the *Aztec* from Tennessee to Long Beach, California to make preparations for the transpacific flight. An additional two-hundred-gallon fuel tank was installed which extended the *Piper Aztec*'s range providing seventeen hours of flight time. With a good wind factor of minus ten or less, the flight to Honolulu would take fifteen hours. Additional equipment was installed including Loran (a long range navigation system) and High Frequency radio.

Our point of departure for the transpacific flight was Oakland with a final inspection by the FAA. I was pleasantly surprised to learn the inspector was Chinese. He was equally surprised to hear Mandarin spoken and that a woman pilot was planning to fly across the ocean. We chatted together in Mandarin as he looked over my documents.

"The documents are all in order and you are well qualified," he said. "Now what about your airplane?"

I was a little concerned at this point and thought, *Could some small item have been overlooked in my preparation?* I waited anxiously as he conducted a thorough and careful check. It seemed like an unusually long time but soon he smiled and shook my hand, "Everything looks good, you're set to go!"

The next morning we received the good news of a wind factor of minus eight. We crawl into the crowded cockpit . . . a large wooden crate crammed against the back of my seat, survival gear under our feet, and life jackets around our necks. I wait for my clearance. *Will this heavy aircraft filled with fuel really make it off the runway?* I wondered. *And what will the controls feel like?*

Suddenly, the radio came to life again, "November 5500 Yankee, you're cleared for takeoff."

The words are loud and clear . . . the words I had been waiting for so many long months to hear. I pushed in the throttle and after what seemed like the longest roll ever experienced, the *Piper Aztec* finally lifted off the runway. We were in the air . . . climbing out with 340 gallons of fuel . . . an unforgettable moment. I soon passed over the Golden Gate Bridge silhouetted against a brightening sky. It's a bridge forever locked in my memory . . . a bridge we sailed *under* on the *Indian Bear* freighter bound for Formosa, and now it's a bridge I am flying *over*. My heart is filled with overwhelming praise for the One who made it all possible.

Because of delays in our flight, we were not able to connect as planned with Richard and Jaime's flight in Hawaii. I radioed ahead to the captain of the Pan Am flight the boys were on asking if he would be willing to relay a message to one of his passengers. He was most accommodating and personally walked back to where Richard was sitting with his little brother, Jaime. Richard looked up in total surprise when the captain spoke to him.

"I was just on the radio with your mother. She wants you to know all is well and that she will see you in Manila. She's not able to meet your flight in Honolulu." It was a special moment for a 13 year-old to talk with a captain and Richard never forgot this exciting encounter.

"We're just up here getting sunburned in the cockpit," the captain radioed back to me. "What are you doing flying over the Pacific?" It was exciting to share our plans for the *Aztec* in the Philippines.

"I enjoyed chatting with your son," he continued. "He's a good babysitter with such a little fellow to care for."

At 2:00 A.M. the brilliant lights of Honolulu came into view. It was such a comforting feeling to see land once again. It had been a long fifteen hours since leaving Oakland making position reports every two-and-a-half degrees. Our average speed was 150 knots with fuel consumption rate of twenty gallons per hour. The flight had gone well and I was happy with the performance of the Aztec. It handled well and I knew it would be a dependable airplane for our mercy flights.

After stopovers on the islands of Majuro, Ponape, Truk, and Yap, we finally reached the Philippines. We could see the top of Mayon volcano, a distant landmark of the Philippines and I knew we were almost to our final destination . . . the Manila International Airport. Although our flight had been delayed out of Yap because of a typhoon, a strong tailwind caused by the typhoon brought us to the Philippines ahead of schedule. I thought that this was why "approach control" had put me in a holding pattern after the long flight. We later learned the real reason . . . preparations for a surprise welcome were still being made.

Upon landing, I taxied behind the "follow me" vehicle and

Philippine Air Force ladies welcome

was directed to a parking area. What an exciting moment to have finally arrived! As we climbed out of the airplane, we were surprised to hear a band playing . . . the Philippine Air Force band greeting us with a hearty welcome. This was followed by a beautiful chorus of Air Force ladies. We were completely overwhelmed, emotionally moved by the warmth of the greetings.

My husband, Bill, with two sons, Richard and Jaime, joined me as the Commanding General of the Philippines Air Force, Jose Rancudo, extended a courteous and friendly welcome. "We are providing you with free fuel for all your flights and want to thank you on behalf of the people of the Philippines for the services you are rendering."

He then added that the Philippine Air Force would be providing tie-down space at their headquarters with personnel to assist in the refueling of the aircraft. All airports would be advised to refuel the *Piper Aztec* without charge.

What an incredible ending to a very long flight! What an en-

Gen. Jose Rancudo greets family

couraging beginning to a mission flying program! My husband and I had begun laying plans for our flights to the islands when an urgent request came from the Commanding General of the PAF.

"Could you help do something for a neglected and distant island of the Philippines . . . Cagayan de Tawi Tawi?" asked General Rancudo.

We were eager to help and accepted the opportunity. This seemingly forgotten island off the coast of Borneo was home to twenty-thousand people and a great deal of uncertainty. "Too dangerous, too far, hostile islanders toward Christians," was the warning. Navigational aids were few and the island was isolated by miles of the Sulu Sea. Leprosy and malignant malaria plagued the islanders. Other tropical diseases remain a constant threat and I was told, "The only good Christian on that island is a dead one." Still the need was there and we made preparations for our flight.

I calculated the flight time to be about an hour and a half in the *Piper Aztec*. Cagayan de Tawi Tawi, like the smaller Turtle

Islands, can easily be overflown if obscured by low lying clouds. Several physicians joined us on this flight. It seemed that my youngest could melt hearts anywhere and Jaime had become a frequent companion on many of my flights.

Tracking out on the Zamboanga VOR navigational aid 270 degrees due west, I corrected for winds. One has to be constantly aware of the wind's predisposition for rapid and frequent fluctuation in the islands. Within a half hour of the island, we began our descent at which time the VOR navigational aid was lost. During the descent, we could only hope for a break in the clouds as we searched for the island. In the final fifteen minutes of the flight, the search became critical.

Suddenly we spotted the island with its carved-out red dirt strip. As we turned to make our approach, we saw a group of tribal men waiting to greet our plane. They were dressed in the costume of the tribal privileged class—some wearing white turbans and others the typical traditional red fez.

Soon after landing, we were warmly welcomed and taken to a large truck which was waiting to take us to our destination—the village of Guppah. With medicines and other supplies in hand, we climbed aboard. We drove over palm branches and coconuts shells as we crisscrossed through a forest of palm trees. Suddenly we arrived in a clearing and saw Guppah, an isolated village, home to many lepers. Soon, the tragic situation was clear. The blind, the disfigured, the helpless, and the hopeless were everywhere. Lying on the floor of one small hut were several small jaundiced children huddled up closely to their delirious mother. A hepatitis epidemic was claiming the lives of young and old alike. Examining three pregnant women seriously ill with hepatitis, we realized that without immediate help, they would not live through the night. I knew they would have to be flown off the

Dr. Wilma and Johnny Talaa direct the clinic

island and hospitalized that night to survive.

It was dark now and there were no lights at the little airstrip. I had not planned to leave until morning but my heart went out to those women whose lives were at stake. Under the circumstances, I felt that the headlights from the truck might give us enough light to take off. By flashlight, we loaded the patients and lifted our hearts in earnest prayer that we would be able to take off. The headlights from the truck shone down the dirt strip, providing just enough light for me to take off.

With thankful hearts for answered prayer, we lift off, airborne with three critically ill women on a flight which is their only hope of survival. Normally, all radios are shut down at night on the island but I picked up a radio beacon thirty minutes out. Zamboanga was soon notified of our flight and arrival time. Our three patients were all on IVs, being monitored by our physician and seemed to be resting quietly.

The flight was going well when suddenly high up in the sky I noticed a bright light at our 12 o'clock position that was descending rapidly. I wondered if it could be a falling star or maybe a meteorite. Soon it was clear that it was on a direct path toward our aircraft. As it came closer, I switched on my landing lights. There was no response. I blinked the lights, but still there was no response. Finally I realized that the light was not turning at all and was rapidly coming closer. I made a sudden and swift turn to the right—a wingover. The brilliant light flashed by us on the left leaving us in total darkness.

I was somewhat shaken but I reassured the physician that all was well. Whatever it was . . . it missed us or we missed it and that was all that mattered for the moment. The physician and patients soon fell back to sleep and I breathed a prayer of gratitude to my heavenly Father for His protecting care. Later I learned that the bright object we avoided that night was a surface-to-air missile.

An hour later we were cleared to land at the airport in Zamboanga, a city on the island of Mindanao. We arranged hospitalization for the three patients who were immediately placed in the Intensive Care Unit. How grateful I am for the medical staff who took such interest in providing care for those extremely sick patients—unknown Muslims from a distant island.

Returning to the island the next morning, we realized the extent of the suffering of these local villagers. Hepatitis and leprosy were serious concerns as well as malignant malaria. A bench set up outdoors became our urgent care clinic as we tried to treat as many patients as possible. There are some who were unable to come and they also needed to be seen. Treating the last patient waiting, I decided to visit one of the village homes, a thatched roof hut supported by wooden stilts. Approaching the entrance to this small dwelling, I hesitated a moment. Outwardly I didn't move but inwardly I faltered. My heart was thrown into deep distress by this disease-deformed spectacle . . . the very antitheses of life. She was seemingly dying while yet breathing. Silent, she squatted in the doorway, her face severely disfigured and fingers clawed by advanced leprosy. I felt utterly helpless and was reminded how our Lord healed the lepers. *Oh, for that miracle touch just now,* I thought. Suddenly the woman moved, slowly rising up on her discolored and toeless feet. There was yet life. She spoke. She motioned and somehow in those blinded eyes gratitude appeared. Then I understood. Before we came, she could only crawl. Now she walks. A nurse's treatments had made the difference.

The islanders—though suffering from disease and impoverished conditions—greeted us with particular kindness and hospitality. Our first visit was followed by numerous follow-up visits and the initial little bamboo clinic soon became a permanent two story structure, housing both the clinic and our physician couple and nurses.

A school which began with dirt floors and coconut log benches was soon transformed into a series of well-built, attractive, hollow block classrooms. The island had a high incidence of hypertension and I discovered that the islanders use sea water for cooking due to the lack of fresh water. ADRA personnel flew with me to the island to determine what help could be provided. Later I flew in a group of engineers who assessed the situation. I was fortunately able to locate a feasibility study done previously and eventually ADRA was able to provide a new well for the city.

Manila Sanitarium and Hospital physicians gave freely of their time and often flew to the island with me to assist in the clinic. The Quiet Hour donated funds for the construction of a chapel. "The long hoped for gift has arrived. We now have funds to build a chapel on land donated by our Muslim friends whose hearts have been touched to see the love and sacrifice made to transform their village and change their children's lives."

How grateful we were for this generous gift from The Quiet Hour. It was a thrill to fly Pastor LaVerne and Alma Tucker in The Quiet Hour's *Wings of Health* airplane to this distant Muslim island. As we arrived at the school in Guppah, we were greeted by the sweet voices of young students singing, "I have decided to follow Jesus." It was a special day we will not soon forget.

There are many who have been instrumental in reaching out to this island. We appreciated the personal interest and support of Pastor Neal Wilson. Students from Weimar College—Bob Hancock Jr. and Byron Corbett—spent a year in Guppah teaching in the fledgling academy and working on a well installation. May Chung visited the island and provided scholarships for graduates of Tawi Tawi Academy to attend CPAC (Central Philippine Adventist College). Several of these students returned later as nurses and teachers to help in the Guppah clinic and Tawi Tawi Academy. It was a very special day of celebration when the government signed a certificate establishing Tawi Tawi Academy as a fully accredited high school.

May Chung, visiting sponsor of Tawi Tawi Academy students.

Physician visits to Tawi Tawi are always an encouragement. Thank you, Dr. Hardinge.

CHAPTER 10
Mercy Missions With the Piper Aztec

The *Piper Aztec*, N5500Y, was approaching the Mountain View College airport, a small grass strip near the college.[1] I had been asked to fly a group of Manobo tribespeople to a nearby island hospital for removal of their goiters. These abnormal enlargements of the thyroid gland are prevalent in the mountain areas.

We had become aware of the needs of the Manobos through the visits of students from the college. Those with goiters had been brought in by jeep from their mountain village and as these

1. An Adventist college on the island of Mindanao

Manobos prepare for flight to the Miller Sanitarium & Hospital in Cebu

Manobos board the airplane, I realize that flying could be a strange and stressful experience for them. Our route would take us over one of the higher mountains and there could be some turbulence. I wanted these tribespeople to understand and not be alarmed by the unusual and sudden movements of the aircraft. I know how frightened they might become having never flown in an airplane before. Even slight turbulence could cause nausea and the need for a sick sack.

Not being able to speak in their language, I go through the motions of buckling their seatbelts. I do this for each of them and then demonstrate the use of the sick sacks. With hand motions, I also show them what to expect as the airplane took off.

We scarcely leave the ground and turn toward the mountains when everything seems to break loose at once. The Manobos all become airsick at the same time using their sick sacks quite forcibly!

Dr. Clarence Ekvall examines a goiter patient

Dr. Manuel Tornilla with his patients after surgery.

Oh no, I think, *this could make it very difficult and uncomfortable for the ones that are pregnant.* One of the women appeared to be pretty close to term in her pregnancy. I could not have imagined that this would happen so soon after takeoff. We were actually in perfectly calm conditions but perhaps it was the stress of riding in an airplane.

What will happen when we really hit turbulence? I begin to wonder. The remainder of the flight, however, goes well, even over the mountains where we do experience some light turbulence. Arriving at the airport in Iligan, we were met by the physicians who would be performing the surgeries. I explain to them my concern over the patients' rather violent reaction to the initial part of the flight. The physicians speak to them for a few minutes and then I noticed broad smiles coming over their faces.

"They thought the use of sick sacks was something they were required to do as part of flying!" one of the physicians exclaims.

"Your sign language must have been quite well understood," another of the physicians added with a smile.

The patients take it in good humor, smiling broadly when it was explained to them. The surgeries were successful and some very happy Manobos, their goiters removed, flew back again in the airplane. I didn't need to demonstrate the use of the sick sack and not one of them became airsick! What a story they had to tell! Not only for the jeep ride, the plane ride, and the surgeries, but also their newfound discovery of sick sacks!

A forgotten little girl of the barrio

I am tired and dirty. Coconut milk and a few bananas still leave room for hunger pangs. The setting sun means that we should soon start our flight back to Manila but the human chain of disease-afflicted bodies presses close around me. One more patient and yet one more. The dense tropical air became cooler with the onset of darkness but the wall of humanity prevents its effects from filtering through. The whole world seems to hang heavy on my flesh. I make a mental note of those still waiting to be seen. Then I see him—a young boy carrying a small child whose face is buried deep into his thin shoulder. He comes cautiously closer as I speak, his eyes wandering from mine to the bundle pressing against him. There is no movement.

Suddenly a frail woman appears and in staccatolike tones shouts at the child. Still there is no movement. She approaches and forces the motionless head upward. The child grimaces and cries and then I see it—the tragedy of a little girl who has every right to be beautiful—her tiny features distorted by the ugliness of a severe harelip. The cry continues and then becomes a steady heart-breaking sob, one which seems to carry with it the woes of all the disadvantaged children in the world.

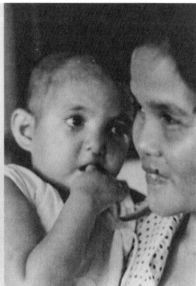

A little girl's harelip is repaired.

I nod understandingly at the woman whose eyes reflect that the bundle is part of her. I motion toward the skies—a gesture which breaks through communication barriers, through the screen of suffering to a flight of hope and healing and beyond to the great Physician who sent angel wings to a forgotten little child of the barrio.

She stares silently upward, then turns and disappears into the thick foliage. I realize that I have to get the other patients to the plane before it gets any later. A threatening sky speaks of possible thunderstorms and I understand too well the hazards of dodging weather at night over the islands. As I turn to leave, the foliage again sprang to life. The woman reappears carrying a small basket. She motions to the boy then lifts the clinging child still sobbing from his shoulder. Gently cradling her, she turns and follows me.

We arrive at our borrowed truck and quickly load the patients. My frequent glances at the darkening skies are less reassuring than the trustful look in the eyes of the weary patients. Soon our little girl cries no longer and falls asleep. Our two and a half hour ride over a rough road leaves time for reflection. *How grateful I am that we have an airplane to transport these seemingly forgotten people of the barrio,* I think.

When we finally arrive at the air strip and patients are loaded, I give a tired but thankful thrust to the throttles and begin our flight to Manila, a flight on "angel wings" for a forgotten little girl from the barrio.

Two weeks later following a successful surgery to close her harelip, the little girl was flown back to her village, not to hide the hurts in darkness anymore, but to a playground of sunshine, a playground of smiles. A place where acceptance in a child's world is instantaneous, where a new life has begun. She can now smile!

Big hope for a small heart

I hold the frail figure close to my heart. Inside this limp form is a heart struggling to keep alive a little 5 year-old girl. I feel its irregular beat and hold her closer. It is a heart with a defect from birth which does not allow the freedom of childhood for this small child, the freedom to run and play like other little girls.

I look down into the sad eyes of a child the same age as my own little Jaime. My heart aches with every beat of that tired heart as I lift her gently into the aircraft. I seem to see her again at 13, confined to a wheelchair and then again at that unfolding, blossoming age of young womanhood, and then later unable to share in the special privilege of motherhood as she is eventually robbed of life itself. *No, this must not happen to this little girl,* I pray. *Oh for the Savior's healing touch!*

Her heart continues its struggle as we fly low over the water. Oxygen is stored next to her father, but we hoped not to have to frighten her with its use. We watch her lips for any signs of cyanosis. Flying low through mountain passes and over the water again I am finally cleared to land at Manila International airport. The ambulance is waiting and the small child is lifted carefully into the ambulance for a ride that hopefully would bring new life to a tiny, tired heart. Surgeons had been notified and once in the hospital, the little girl waits for that miracle touch. As I watch her lying there on clean, white sheets of the hospital bed, I lift up a silent prayer that the great Physician would touch yet another life.

The miracle did happen and months later I returned with the *Wings of Health* aircraft. This is the flight I always look forward to

A little girl's mercy flight

. . . one that brings back to a village a restored life and knowledge of the One who makes it all happen. The smiles, the joy, the homecoming . . . these were not soon forgotten!

The best birthday gift ever!

The little Muslim boy is placed on the operating table. A large congenital growth protrudes from his forehead severely disfiguring his young face. We had encouraged his parents to allow him to come with us for what could be his only hope of living a normal life or even living at all. We had flown him from the island of Cagayan de Tawi Tawi off the coast of Borneo to the Miller Sanitarium and Hospital in Cebu.

This had been our first visit to the all Muslim island in the Sulu Sea and our hearts went out to this little boy. Anxious parents did permit us to take him with us. The surgeon, Dr. Manuel

Sister carries brother for flight to Cebu

Tornilla, evaluated the child and felt an operation was possible. This was a very critical situation as we were trying to demonstrate our concern for these Muslim people. They had put their trust in us, allowing their little boy to fly far from home not knowing what the outcome would be. Somehow we felt that this was our one and only opportunity to show our love for these people. We realized that flying back without a living child might forever close the door to this island for our medical team.

As was his custom, Dr. Tornilla prayed before the operation. He then began the delicate surgical procedure, on this little boy . . . a very difficult and challenging operation. Suddenly the child arrested—his heart stopped. Just as suddenly, Dr. Tornilla in an earnest plea spoke a prayer that everyone could hear.

"Lord, please bring back a heartbeat . . . I ask for nothing else today . . . on my birthday but the life of this little boy."

There wasn't a dry eye in that operating room. It seemed every heart was reaching out to the little boy. Then it happened. Efforts were not in vain. The heart quivered and started beating again. God in His mercy was answering the prayer of this faithful Christian physician, the only gift he desired on his birthday. The operation was successful and we had the privilege of flying this little boy back to his island home. Oh, the joy of those Muslim parents in seeing the healed face of their little boy.

"Why, he's beautiful!" they exclaimed. God answered a physician's prayer and opened the door to the hearts of these Muslim people.

"Yes, please come back to help the other children," pleaded the mothers. Their trust was instantaneous and we have promised to return.

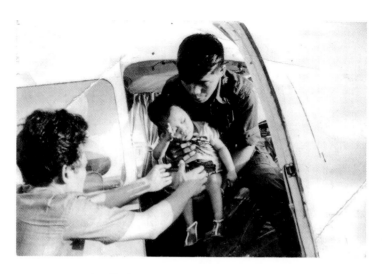

The flight to save a little boy's eyesight

Operation baby lift

It was children's day in the little barrio of Bacacay. This small village lies at the foot of Mayon volcano where a group of parents searched the skies, waiting for the arrival of the airplane that will take their children for much needed surgery. Some of the children waiting to be airlifted look but cannot see, some can see but do not hear, and one is too weak to even stand. But they all know that a plane is arriving . . . their very first plane ride which will help them to walk again, to see again, to hear again. Parents of these children sense the deeper meaning of a new life for them. The *Wings of Health* airplane has become a common sight flying into the Legaspi airport, not only bringing patients for medical care but also to assist in the aftermath of devastating typhoons. This region is well know for the unusually sever typhoons that strike the area.

Flying alongside the volcano, I throttle back as I approached the village. I begin to circle . . . the signal telling those waiting that

Critically ill infant restored to health

we'll soon be there to pick up the children. This arrangement had been made the week before when each child's condition was assessed. As I near the airport, I hear a call from a Philippine Airline pilot telling approach control to allow 5500 Yankee in first. "She's probably picking up some more patients," the captain of the PAL flight radioed. There is no emergency on this particular flight, but I thank the captain for his concern. There were times when it actually was an emergency and the PAL flights were most courteous in accommodating under these conditions.

It's always a satisfying feeling to be able to return patients to their village homes . . . little ones with a new heart, better vision and hearing restored. How grateful I am for the opportunity to make a difference in these little one's lives.

As Christ told His disciples, "Suffer little children to come unto me, and forbid them not for such is the kingdom of heaven" (Matthew 19:14).

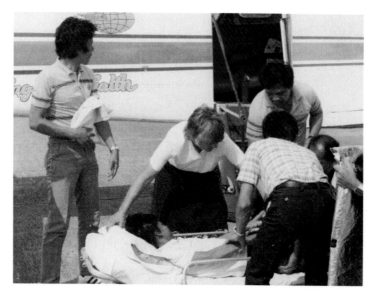

Joel being transported to Wings of Health *for flight to Manila Sanitarium & Hospital*

"Joel will not die!"

Joel was not expected to live much longer. He had been diagnosed with a fatal form of cancer and was thought to be in the terminal stages of the disease. I had flown the *Wings of Health* airplane to the island of Palawan where Health Expo meetings were being held by The Quiet Hour. It was there that the young man, Joel, had caught the attention of our team. His family requested special prayer and Pastor Laverne Tucker asked if I would visit Joel to determine if anything could be done for him.

Invited to his room, I found Joel curled up in a fetal position waiting to die. I learned what the local doctors had reported about his condition and the picture looked very grim. "No hope" seemed to be written on every fiber of this thin young man's body. Somehow I couldn't help but feel that there was hope. The

Joel restored to health

diagnosis did not seem to really fit his condition. I was impressed after praying for Joel that if at all possible we should fly him to our Manila Sanitarium and Hospital for a more definitive diagnosis. Yes, we could take Joel on a stretcher to the plane and on to the Manila International Airport where an ambulance would be waiting to bring him to the hospital. The physicians had agreed to see him for evaluation and perhaps admit this special patient for treatment.

After a thorough examination and extensive testing, it was determined that Joel did not have cancer. What wonderful news for his family! His disease was treatable and the Manila Sanitarium and Hospital offered to keep this young man for extended therapy. Joel, who could hardly sit up, began to get stronger and soon was able to walk. After some months of treatment, Joel's health improved and he was sponsored as a student at Mountain View College. Along with his class work, he worked on the farm there, growing stronger every day.

"No, Joel will not die but live!" God had other plans for this young man's life.

Erie's new voice

"Erie, get your things together and come with us. I believe at Loma Linda you can be successfully operated on." Erie had a serious harelip and cleft palate problem which local doctors had not been able to repair.

I first met Erie during the Better Living Crusade in Davao, Mindanao, where we joined Pastor Robert Spangler of the General Conference in a blended health and gospel ministry. Erie, the janitor boy, lived in the basement sleeping quarters of our local church. He could hardly be understood because of his serious physical problem but he loved to sing as he swept and cleaned the rooms each morning. The pitiful nasal sounds were not so pleasant to the ear, but we could feel the contagious joy and praise . . . he seemed so full of happiness in spite of his affliction.

Overjoyed at the invitation, Erie put together his few things and flew with us across the Pacific to our home in Loma Linda, California. I brought Erie to the Loma Linda Medical Center to see Dr. Tom Zirkle, who had kindly offered to help. Upon examination, he found a very severe cleft palate abnormality which would take a series of surgeries to correct. Erie stayed with us for a year while Dr. Zirkle and his staff performed the needed surgeries.

The day finally came when the last of the series of operations was performed. The surgeries were a complete success and Erie returned home with a new life . . . a new voice to sing praises to His Lord! How grateful we were to Dr. Tom Zirkle, his staff and Loma Linda Medical Center for providing this remarkable change in Erie's life. No longer hard to understand, Erie became a Sabbath School teacher. As the years passed, Erie studied construction, married a minister's daughter and was employed as builder for the mission.

The *Wings of Health* airplane came to Erie's home town. Our team presented the first Health Expo to be held there attended by a large and responsive audience. With understandable pride, Erie took us on a tour of the chapels he had built. Many of these chapels had been funded by The Quiet Hour. They were well built and each one had a distinctive and attractive trim.

"Erie, where did you ever get all these ideas for building?" we asked, amazed at this former janitor boy's abilities.

"I remembered many of the things I saw when I was in California, and I studied so I could be a builder for God." Erie answered.

Erie, builder of churches, was also a builder of men. He left his mark on the many lives he touched. From a janitor boy who could hardly speak to one who patterned his life after the Master builder, Erie Bacomo shared his new life with clarity. Erie today is resting from his labors but his beloved companion continues to carry on what this builder for God shared so deeply in his own life for Christ.

When God cleared the runway!

It was an unforgettable day for the *Wings of Health* aircraft. My heart was filled with gratitude for the One who made the flights possible. Yes, He's always with me on my flights but that day His presence seemed especially near. A flight plan to Cagayan de Oro in the South had been filed, and waiting at the airport would be a welcoming committee from the Southern Philippine Union Mission. This was a special day in which their church world leader, his wife and the treasurer would be visiting the mission for some special meetings. As the mission group waited, their hopes of the visitor's actual arrival became more and more uncertain. They soon learn that because of threatening weather, the PAL (Philippine Airline) flight for that day had been cancelled.

In the distance the *Piper Aztec*, N5500Y, with the visitors aboard, would soon be approaching the airport. I had been briefed of the weather conditions and realized an instrument approach would most likely be necessary. Threatening thunder clouds confirmed this.

"It appears we will need to make an instrument approach," I explained to the passengers as we entered the clouds. Soon I learned that even an instrument approach might not be possible. The airport was now covered with clouds and any landing seemed totally out of the question. Taking the aircraft down out of the clouds into VFR conditions, I looked for any breaks in the cloud layer ahead. Before turning back to Cebu, I felt that if God wanted us to land, He would provide a way. Flying low over the water, I suddenly saw an incredible sight! Straight ahead, a lighted path of sunshine led directly down from the sky and over the entire length of the runway. The only view in sight was the sunlit runway sandwiched between dark storm clouds on either side. It seemed God had carved a brilliant path of His glory opening up the heavens for our little aircraft.

"N5500Y, you're cleared to land," said the rather astonished voice from the control tower. We were the only aircraft approaching the airport that day to hear those words!

Soon after we touched down and taxied to the ramp, the torrential rains began to fall. And there in the rain stood a very amazed and delighted group of greeters. Stepping out of the plane, Pastor and Mrs. Neal Wilson with Brother Lance Butler were met by a jubilant group with umbrellas for all. "Not even the PAL planes could get in," remarked one overjoyed greeter. Surely this was God's doing! *Thank you, my heavenly Father, for yet another miracle in our* Wings of Health *ministry.*

God changed my flight plan!

The persistent ringing of the telephone awakened me unusually early one morning. The voice on the other end sounded anxious and hurried. "Could you please fly our medical team to Baler . . . today?" It was one of the physicians from the Manila Sanitarium and Hospital. Hesitating, he then added, "We realize it's a last minute request but it's really very urgent."

A *C-47* which could carry their team of thirty people had been assigned to the medical group by the Philippine Air Force. However two hours before departure time, the promised plane was

not able to make it. The physicians with their equipment were ready to leave. Surgeries had been promised to patients who had hiked several days down rough mountain trails to reach the hospital in Baler. This capital city of Aurora Sub-Province is nearly seven hours from Manila using difficult and at times treacherous overland transportation. Special flights, however, can be arranged that take less than an hour through the Sierra Madre mountain range.

"How many are on board for the flight," I asked, "and how much equipment?" Quickly I had calculated that with the six available seats in the Twin *Piper Aztec,* it would take three round trips through the pass making a total of approximately six hours flying time. It would be a challenge to fly all the physicians and equipment there in time for the scheduled surgeries, but I had never turned down a request. "I'll be ready to board the first group in one hour" I replied.

The physician immediately notified the Lieutenant Governor of Baler who would be waiting at the airport with transportation for the team. Flight plans were filed for November 5500 Yankee and the first group of doctors and nurses with the anesthesiology machine were boarded. With the weight and balance in the aircraft carefully calculated, I placed the heavier physician in the front passenger seat. It was a full load.

A weather briefing and contact with the governor in Baler assured us of clear visibility along our route as well as at the airport. However as we were ready to depart, a last minute check of the weather brought an unexpected change in my flight plan. Thunderstorm activity with large buildups had suddenly developed in the Sierra Madres, creating hazardous flying conditions through the pass. Pilots were reporting that the pass was literally "socked in." It was disappointing and very unusual as this kind of buildup

N5500Y road landing at Baler

is seen mostly in the afternoons. I filed another flight plan on another route where only a few scattered showers were expected.

As we approached Baler, we could see the airport was completely clouded over. I had to make a decision: we either needed to land at another alternate airport or find a road straight and wide enough to land the *Aztec*. There was no airport near enough to be of any practical use, so I turned my attention to a road which might be possible to put the twin down on. I soon noticed a straight road leading from the overcast airstrip to the town. Regulations require a pilot to circle three times to alert any on a highway that a plane is coming down. As I circled the final time to land on the road, I tipped a wing to avoid some coconut palms before touching down.

At that moment, the physician seated next to me lost all his breakfast—the contents of which totally frosted the instrument panel! A nurse behind him reached over and frantically tried to

clean up some of the instruments. Quickly wiping off the airspeed indicator, I dodged the last palm tree and touched down with just enough space on the road for the wheels and no interference for the wings. Our airsick surgeon was the first to climb out of the plane. His recovery was rapid, however, and one hour later he was in the operating room performing surgery on his first patient!

The welcoming group who had been waiting at the airport with Lieutenant Governor Etcubanez soon arrived. The governor had cancelled all of his conflicting appointments so that he could stay with the team while they were in town.

Other members of the hospital's medical team had been traveling for a week by land transportation. Now, they were concerned whether they would make it for the first surgery scheduled at 2:00 P.M. that day. Their trip had become extremely dangerous—at the entrance to the Sierra Madre Mountain range, a landslide completely blocked traffic. *How could they get through?* they wondered. It seemed only divine intervention could make this possible. They prayed. They waited. Before long, a bulldozer arrived and was able to clear the area. In 30 minutes, they were on their way once again. As they neared Baler, they noticed heavy clouds over the airport area and wondered whether the plane carrying their team would be able to land. As they watched the clouds, our plane suddenly appeared, seeming to drop out of the skies on the road directly in front of them. Surprised and overjoyed, they could hardly believe what they were seeing. They had arrived in time to join the welcoming party that had come from the airport to meet our plane!

Realizing I must return quickly for the next group of physicians, I estimate the remaining length of the road for takeoff. More space will be needed and officers kindly assist in pushing the plane back to where it had touched down. They cleared the road, holding back the traffic—tricycles, motorbikes, jeepneys and carts—with officers at each end. I taxi down the road, my narrow "runway," building up speed, V1, V2, and ready for liftoff. As the plane comes close to where the officers are standing at the far end of the road the officers begin frantically pointing their thumbs heavenward! It seems they think I have forgotten I'm in an airplane and not a car. With a safe airspeed I soon lift off and return for the next group of physicians. It is arranged for my next flight that these same officers will block the road again making it unnecessary for me to circle.

With most of the supplies, medicines, and instruments—including the anesthesiology machine—brought in on the first flight, the team was immediately able to set up for the surgeries. They made more space for surgery by turning the delivery and treatment room in the dispensary into operating rooms. The first patient was prepped for the operation and then there was a pause. One of the surgeons offered a word of prayer before beginning the operation. This was something new to the non "Sabadistas." The government nurses opposite the surgeon leaned forward to hear every word he was saying.

This wooden-frame government hospital had provisions for only twenty-five beds. With this surgical mission team, the demand swelled to seventy-five which meant that the entire hallway had to be filled with various kinds of beds. On the last day of the surgeries, the patients who lived nearby had to bring their own beds in addition to the needed bedding which patients normally bring.

In returning with the second group of physicians, I discovered strong crosswinds over the road. They were beyond the maximum winds for a crosswind landing in the *Aztec.* So I turned toward the airstrip to discover that the winds had cleared away the clouds. Soon after our landing, the welcoming committee appeared with the governor again. The governor remarked in surprise, "When we're at the airport you land on the road. When we're at the road you land at the airport! Where will you land next?"

"Wherever it is the safest," I explained. I thanked the Lord there was a road when needed and was just as thankful for clear skies over the little airstrip.

Returning to Baler on our final flight, I noticed a group of soldiers standing on the airstrip. I decided to make a fly over to make sure it was clear to land. I then saw the soldiers waving me down and clearing me for landing. After we touched down and secured the aircraft, we were immediately hurried to the hospital. As the governor approached me, he pointed to the skies saying, "There must be somebody up there looking out for you!" He then told me of a serious situation which had developed with a particular rebel group. They had blockaded a road and ambushed several buses. Violence had erupted and submachine guns had been set up by the rebels. They were ready to fire at the first plane coming through the pass, knowing the Philippine Air Force would be called in. We all realized that our plane would have been the first to fly through the pass had it not been for the sudden change of weather. "Yes," I told the governor, "there is somebody up there looking out for us. He changed my flight plan!"

One touching scene will always be rememberd. Two young sisters ages five and six had harelips. They were among those who had to be turned down due to lack of time, yet their father never gave up hope that somehow they might have the needed surgery. Not only did the father have the patience to stand by the operating room for two days but also the ability to persuade the girls to be willing to have the operation. He finally won the children's confidence upon the presentation of new face towels which they immediately used to wipe away their tears. At last the father's faith and perseverance were rewarded. Just before the team had to leave, the father got his wish. Two of the surgeons gently placed them on the operating tables. Within two hours, their harelips were repaired and still bandaged as the physicians boarded the helicopter for their return to Manila.

Helicopters were provided by the PAF to assist in flying out the physicians which made it convenient for only one flight to be made in the *Aztec*. After four days of surgeries the team had operated on fifty-six patients—forty-three cases of thyroidectomies, seven harelips, and six minor cases before they had to leave. The governor invited the "Sabadistas" to return, "We want you to come back soon. Build your clinic, your school, your church . . . anytime. I am deeply grateful for the kind of humanitarian work you are doing unselfishly for the poor and unfortunate people of this sub-province."

"It isn't safe to stay here."

On one of my flights in the *Wings of Health* an interesting story unfolded. The island, Limasawa, was hard hit by typhoon, "Nitang" and what appeared to be once a little airstrip, fallen branches had totally disguised. On this flight with me was Pastor Peter Niere, the president of the Central Philippine Union Mission. As we surveyed the damage, he related a remarkable experience that had just happened.

A church elder lived on this island with his wife. One night he was awakened by a dream. He soon realized it might not be a dream as he heard a voice speaking to him. The voice was telling him he must leave his home. He wasn't sure that he had heard right and so fell back to sleep. However the voice came again and this time he wakened his wife telling her about the voice that seemed so urgent. She felt he must not be feeling well to be hearing voices and suggested he go back to sleep. The voice came stronger the third time and he told his wife. "We must not wait longer. We must leave now."

This time she believed him. Picking up his lantern, the elder prepared to leave the village with his wife. As they walked along, he thought to himself, *If I was warned to leave, then I should also tell all the other people in the village.*

As he walked past the other houses, he called out to them, "You must leave now, it isn't safe to stay here." Because the man was known in the village as a very sincere and honest man, many villagers believed and came out to follow him. Holding his lamp high, he continued up the mountainside with nearly five-hundred men, women and children following. The palm branches were blowing and bowing almost to the ground. The group walked up to the church which was midway up the mountain but it was not large enough to hold them all. Then the church elder noticed the hollow blocks in the wall moving strangely. He felt it was not safe to stay and called out, "We must go up the mountain further. Do not stay here." The people continued to follow the elder with the lamp up the mountain.

Meanwhile back in the village, a mother with her small baby could not get ready in time to follow the others. But she felt she should leave and so she walked up the hillside alone. It was dark but she could see the violent swaying of the palm trees. Frightened by the increasingly strong winds, she arrived at the church and rushed inside for protection, crouching under the pulpit as she held her baby tightly.

The crowd who had gone ahead had now reached the top of the mountain. They waited there for the sound of the winds to let up. It seemed an eternity before the storm passed over but finally the church elder felt it was safe to return to their homes. As the group approached the church, they stopped in astonishment. There was no church. Only the pulpit was still standing. And inside the pulpit were the mother and baby, frightened but safe. She joined them as they continued down the hill through the debris of palm branches and fallen trees.

They soon arrived back at their village. But there was no village . . . only strewn pieces of Nipa shingles and broken bits of furniture. Coming to the shoreline, they found the bodies of those who had remained behind. Sadly more than fifty had lost their lives but nearly five-hundred had heeded the call from the godly man with the lamp.

We circled the island but could not find a place to land. Hopefully it will not be long before the little airstrip is cleared for the *Wings of Health* to safely land and bring in the much-needed supplies.

CHAPTER 11
The Rescue

For how long my thoughts continued in this filmstrip of reflections I do not know; but as darkness real and seemingly forever closes in around me, my eyes are momentarily directed upward. Just twelve hours earlier, we had flown in confidence and comfort on those highways in the skies. Again the promise comes to me, "Whatsoever believing ye shall receive" (Matthew 21:22). Yes, I believe that someday a rescue will come in a blaze of glory. That's what matters most to me now. I want to be part of that final rescue. My eyes seem fastened to the skies as I continue to lift them upward. Cold and tired I seem paralyzed in thought . . . when suddenly I am attracted to a faint glow in the East. I seem to see a brightening of the horizon. *Could it be real? Perhaps it's only a mirage or my inner self-wishing?* I try to focus and then I begin to see it more clearly . . . a tiny light is emerging though the clouds and slowly edging its way toward the west. Yes, it's there and it's for real!

"Look! That must be the helicopter," exclaims Aubrey, the reality confirmed by the unusually bright tone of his voice.

Suddenly the thoughts of a five-day ordeal vanish swiftly into

Sea King Rescue Helicopter

the awareness of an immediate rescue. The small light shining out of the East continues toward the West . . . and then turns back again. We realize they must be doing a line search.

Aubrey bolts toward the aircraft and switches on the radios. *Doesn't he know they must be frozen,* I'm thinking. Then we hear it! That so-often irritating clatter to a pilot's ears—static—suddenly sounds heavenly. Above it all comes the reassuring words, "We've got them now. They're OK—uh—they're OK and around a fire."

The animation of that voice reflects our own enthusiasm that rescue is imminent. "Whatsoever ye shall ask in my name, believing ye shall receive," yes, His promises are sure.

The distant light soon merges into a larger one, illuminating what we know to be the bright orange surface of the helicopter. Approaching closer, it circles once, makes a final pass, then turns and hovers about twenty yards from our position. The swirling snow stirred up by the helicopter's prop wash creates a fairylike atmosphere. Three giant figures emerge framed in fur—our rescuers! They rush down the air stair door as the big ship hovers.

The thrill of that moment is beyond expression. Hoping to capture it, I reach for my movie camera. The battery is dead, the controls frozen and useless. Then finding my 35 mm camera, I fumble for the shutter release, but the constant cold has taken its toll. This priceless moment will have to remain only in memory; the stoic face of the Arctic alone witnessing this emotion-packed scene.

I glance up from the camera, and peer into the bewildered faces of the rescuers who had every intention of carrying two half-frozen pilots to safety "not a couple of tourists!" they exclaim in complete surprise.

Setting down my camera, I motion that all is well.

With our rescue team!

"I can make it." I confidently state.

My stiffened muscles feel as if I'm walking on stilts. My legs are numb . . . seemingly frozen in place as I try to move them. A strong arm wraps itself around me and escorts me over the ice and through the blinding snow created by the prop wash from the helicopter. Communication at this time is neither possible, nor necessary as we share the common bond pilots have for one another—irrespective of color, creed, or nationality. My eternal thanks to these angels from the shores of Greenland and the skies of Denmark! One downed American pilot of Norwegian descent will not soon forget.

My tense muscles begin to relax as I sit in the security and warmth of the helicopter. For the first time in twelve hours, aching muscles become limp and breathing is effortless again. As the helicopter hovers, I am completely lost in the reverie of rescue. I am a person with a future again, surrounded by security and the compassion of man . . . a God-given gift seen at its best in reaching out to another suffering human being,

As the dulling effects of the cold wear off, I begin to realize all that was left behind in the plane . . . a favorite Bible, passport, logbook, cameras, tape recorder and a much treasured stethoscope having listened to many little hearts in the Philippines. I must go back and retrieve these valuables. Having spent fifteen years traveling in the Orient, I knew the immediate need for a passport . . . any further traveling will require it. One of the crew offers to go back and recover the items.

I realize however that it will be next to impossible for him to fit his six foot frame into the small area by the ferry tank. Together we walk back through the swirling, blinding snow created by the prop wash from the helicopter.

Once inside the aircraft I quickly look for my Bible, passport,

Oh the joy of being rescued!

cameras, and other valuables. I'm so grateful for the help of this crew member as I continue to hand him as many items I can find. With arms full of all that I can manage to pull out of the cabin we trudge back over the ice again through the blinding snow and prop wash. Once inside the helicopter I suddenly remember the traveler's checks I had set aside for fuel costs. I know just where the $1,500 booklet of checks is hidden and I must go back for it. This time Aubrey joins us. Finding the traveler's checks and Aubrey's small suitcase, we return to the helicopter once again. Aubrey decides to unzip his suitcase to include an item while unconsciously walking under the prop wash of the helicopter. He realizes his mistake too late as the entire contents of the suitcase take flight . . . socks, shorts, shirts, toiletries and papers are scattered in every direction over the ice beyond reach! He stares a moment in disbelief and then climbs into the helicopter holding his empty suitcase. It was a sad moment and one of complete helplessness. I think our rescuers were trying to hold back some smiles.

The helicopter lifts off and as the rotors turn so do my thoughts. I whisper a prayer of gratitude as I look back at the aircraft, not only for our rescue and our rescuers, but also a heavenly Father directing it all.

The helicopter circles over our little "place" . . . a place that seems hallowed for the moment . . . a place to be forever identified in our logbooks. No longer just coordinates on a chart but a real place . . . all twelve inches of God's care and mercy! We say a final farewell to *Lake 1107 Lima* as we circle once more.

"Will I ever see her again?" I wonder.

Aboard the helicopter, we begin to feel extremely thirsty. We ask for water but are told they only have hot drinks on board. I felt plain water would quench thirst the best but grateful at this point for anything liquid. A hot drink is provided for each of us which we are told is specifically for survivors rescued off the ice.

I was so overcome with thirst that I drank the entire cup though somewhat bitter. Yet it was liquid and I was thankful for it. I soon asked for another and still one more before settling back to get some much needed rest. It was such a comfortable feeling to be able to lie quietly after so many tense hours of constant movement to stay alive.

What's going wrong with me? I wonder to myself as I begin to feel restless and somewhat nauseated. I can't understand when I wanted so much to rest why I was becoming so agitated. One of the crew members notices and brought me a pan.

This is a fine time to get sick, I thought. Then my mind turned to the drink. Perhaps just too many cups all at once. I asked Aubrey if he knew what was in the drink.

"That was strong black coffee to keep people alive," he replied with a grin.

I had never used coffee and in fact had never even tasted it, but it certainly more than revived one tired survivor!

Will I ever see her again?

CHAPTER 12
"Good Morning, Holsteinborg!"

I waken. I wonder. Unfamiliar sights and sounds press in around me. Earlier events seem momentarily erased by the silence of the past forty-eight hours. I recognize nothing. Looking down at myself, I discover I am fully clothed. The odor of burnt fuel suddenly quickens my memory and my ordeal begins to unravel. Yes, this must be Greenland.

Catching sight of a small wash basin in the corner of my room I pull myself together. I walk toward the mirror which is hanging above the basin. The next few moments will be etched forever in my memory. I stare into the mirror, scarcely believing what I see. The whites of my eyes and my teeth are the only parts of me that seem to belong. I search to find myself—somewhere behind a layer of what appears to be red dye. Finding a bar of soap I begin to scrub. I scrub harder, but the red dye remains. I discover some cleanser, but with all the scrubbing, the redness seems to only intensify. My winter boots are covered with red dye, as is my hair, my parka and my hands.

Seeing the only window in the room I walk over to look out. What I see is truly a fairyland as the rising sun brings color and

life to a sleeping village.

"Good morning, Holsteinborg!" I call out. Smoke belches from chimneys on steep-roofed houses. A quaint village is wakening; the movement of men and dog sleds stir up flurries of freshly fallen snow. Grabbing my camera to capture this incredible scene, I start down the hallway.

As I make my way down a flight of stairs I hear an unfamiliar language. A woman behind a reception desk is greeting me. All smiles, she hands me a jar of cream and motions that it will remove the redness. I discover it merely helps soothe the rawness from the scrubbing. The red dye remains. *Where is Aubrey?* I wonder. I inquire but am unable to make myself understood. The woman shrugs helplessly.

I step cautiously out the door. Ice appears everywhere. A church's snow-covered steeple—the main landmark of the quiet, lovely village—is silhouetted against the brightening skies. A dog sled carrying a child passes by. Another husky dog is wandering

loose, dragging his rope and he decides to follow this curious stranger. We walk together down by the edge of the shoreline where the remains of frozen boat hulls lie half-buried in the snow. Not until later do I learn that these huskies, away from their sleds, can be potentially dangerous. It seems that the dog and I suffer from a similar problem, both of us wandering, one from a dog sled and one from a crippled airplane, neither of us quite aware of where we are going.

My camera starts functioning again after the freeze on the ice floe and I am thrilled to be able to capture some of the beauties of this unique place. The husky finally turns and walks the other way. I remain a few more minutes, gazing at the unique and un-usual charm of my surroundings. Soon, too soon, the relentless frigid air forces a quick retreat from the quaint village streets.

There is nothing I recognize about my surroundings and I re-member very little of even being brought to this place. I do recall

and marvel that the car we were riding in was able to keep from skidding over the ice.

Inside the hostel, I find Aubrey in conversation with a gentleman. This stranger has offered to take us by car to purchase helicopter tickets for a flight to Sondestrom. We learn that we had been sleeping in this seaman's quarters for more than twenty-four hours straight. Such was our exhausted condition upon arrival. We are then taken to the same helicopter station where we had arrived the day before. As curious people stare, I seem to feel the red dye burying itself permanently into my skin.

"Tell me, why does white squaw wear red paint on face?" asked one of the Eskimo women to the helicopter pilot.

I learn from his answer the cause of the redness. A box of red dye had been included in the drop from the *DC3* captain normally used to identify the location of downed pilots. I had torn open the cardboard box to use for the fire. Unknowingly the contents were being constantly transferred from my gloves to my face as I wiped away freezing tears from my eyes.

Boarding the helicopter, we soon arrive in Sondestrom. We attempt to explain our situation to the officials at the airport but neither us knew any Danish. We were finally able to make contact with Sondestrom Air Force personnel who were aware of our circumstances.

"There is a Sabreliner jet coming in to refuel within fifteen minutes," advised Sondestrom. "They are returning to the United States from Saudi Arabia and might assist you as they have an empty plane."

This was good news, but my concern was how to get out to the fuel pumps. I could not speak Danish and certainly would be misunderstood trying to reach an aircraft being refueled. Security would surely stop me. The Sabreliner soon landed and began taxiing to the fuel pumps. Here was my opportunity! I prayed not to be noticed and started walking in the direction of the Sabreliner. I thought if only I could reach the captain before being stopped by security he would bring us aboard with no questions asked. I reach the aircraft and start up the air stair door just as the captain is coming down. He stares in complete bewilderment as I blurt out, "Captain, please excuse me, but my plane went down on the ice. Do you think you could help two stranded pilots get back to America?" He appears to want to give me the world at this point and replied in astonishment, ". . . . ! Bring whatever and whoever you have and come." We had thought previously that we would have to purchase tickets on SAS (Scandinavian Airlines) through Europe in order to get home to America.

I rush back to tell Aubrey and we quickly gather what little we have salvaged from the *Lake Amphibian*. We then board what

Arrival with the Twin Bonanza *at Redlands Airport . . .*
"Thank you, Pastor Tucker and The Quiet Hour."

surely must be the Cadillac of the skies—a Rockwell Sabreliner jet. Two jet pilots graciously fly us to Syracuse, New York, and on to Saint Louis, Missouri. They invite me to sit in the jump seat and I stare at an amazing "state of the art" instrument panel. All gauges are in the normal operating range and yes, a normal oil pressure reading! Once again we sit in comfort looking down at the frozen world below. My gratitude to the captain of that ship!

Two days later we learned that the *Lake Amphibian* had drifted sixteen miles south and been broken up by pressure from moving ice ridges. This was indeed a disappointment but I was confident there would be another plane, another opportunity for a mission yet to be accomplished, yet to be fulfilled. Somewhere a plane is waiting and those distant isles shall not have waited in vain.

It wasn't long after returning home that I received a phone call from Pastor LaVerne Tucker. "Dorothy, could you use a *Twin Bonanza* airplane?" Pastor Tucker asked. "It's based in Portland, Oregon, and needs new engines. If you think you could use it, we'll provide the new engines, but you'll need to get it down here some way."

How quickly God does answer prayers, I thought to myself. I was not really familiar with the *Beechcraft Twin Bonanza (D50C)* but I quickly said, "Yes, of course." I had been praying earnestly after losing the *Lake Amphibian* that God would supply another airplane . . . just the right one to replace the *Lake*. Recognizing the high time on the engines of the *Twin Bonanza*, I asked Aubrey, an experienced mechanic, to accompany me. Arriving at the Portland airport we find Jack Lange, the owner, waiting for us. I was delighted to see the spacious cabin which seemed ideal for our mission flights and onboard treatment of patients. Aubrey checked over the aircraft documents and other than the high time on the engines, the aircraft appeared well maintained. I flew around the pattern with Jack to become familiar with the characteristics of this particular twin and then we were on our way.

I was very happy with the performance of the airplane as we continued our flight to California. Nearing the city of Bakersfield, I suddenly lost the right engine—it abruptly failed. It couldn't have happened at a more convenient time as the runway lights at the Bakersfield airport were directly ahead. I was cleared for a "straight-in" approach.

After several days in Bakersfield, mechanics completed the repairs on the engine. It seemed the old adversary was not happy with losing just one mission aircraft, just one aircraft engine; he was after another. As I was approaching the Redlands airport, the other engine failed. I was thankful after the failure of both engines to finally land the *Twin Bonanza* at our destination airport.

New engines were soon installed and the aircraft prepared for its transpacific flight to the Philippines. How grateful we were for answered prayer and this one more miracle made possible by Pastor LaVerne Tucker and The Quiet Hour ministry.

Dedication of the *Twin Bonanza*

It was a day of celebration. The newly arrived *Twin Bonanza* sat on the tarmac at the Manila International Airport in full view of the many who had come to witness the special dedication of the aircraft, N245AG. Physicians involved in the Medical Aviation Program participated in the unique service. Both government and nongovernment personnel, along with representatives from the Philippine Air Force, were present at the unusual ceremony: the dedication of an airplane, *Wings of Health*. Special guests included Pastor LaVerne and Alma Tucker from The Quiet Hour.

Visitors enjoyed an "inside look" at the aircraft with its spacious cabin and unique design. The air stair entry door, three rows of seats, air conditioning and large baggage area makes it ideally suited for transportation and onboard treatment of patients. The structurally sound aircraft had also been used by the military and is well suited for the kinds of airstrips used in our medical flights. What a blessing this specially designed aircraft will be in bringing health and healing to the Philippine islands.

Dedication of N245AG by Pastor LaVerne Tucker

Wings of Health *enroute to Cagayan de Tawi Tawi*

CHAPTER 13
Wings of Health *on Call*

"We need your help urgently," the message read, "Mayon Volcano has erupted again!" Our family soon learned that seventy-five thousand people had been displaced by the violent eruption and were now in evacuation centers. It all happened so suddenly that food had become scarce and the needs overwhelming. We also learned that another typhoon, Nitang, had also hit, leaving several hundred thousand people without homes in fifteen islands of the Philippines. It was the worst typhoon on record yet to hit the Visayas. [1]

We quickly organized our group and with the ADRA team, loaded the *Wings of Health* with food and clothing for the flight. I filed a flight plan directly to Legaspi, the nearest city to the erupting volcano. Church and government agencies alike were answering the calls for emergency aid. This series of disasters had literally paralyzed the entire region.

Approaching the city of Legaspi in the *Twin Bonanza*, I saw in the distance the billowing ash spewing from the volcano. It is an alarming sight, realizing what lay below. We could only imagine

---

1. The Visayas are an island group in the Philippines.

Ready to depart for Tawi Tawi—from left to right— the Air Marshall, Ben Sumicad, Pilot Dorothy, Don Von Ornam, Milton Neblett, Engie Domondon, and Delfin Pingol.

the destruction from the lava covering everything in its path as it flows down the mountainside. The tragedy of it all staggers the mind. Nearing the airport and so thankful the ash is not blowing toward it, I continued my approach. Soon I received the clearance, "November 245 Alpha Gulf, you're cleared to land." A Philippine Airline flight had just landed and both of us taxied to the far end of the runway where it seemed much less likely that ash would fall. We understood too well the disastrous effect ash could have on the engines of our aircraft.

Our team of physicians and ADRA personnel were soon met by mission staff and transported to the area where supplies would be distributed. As we drew near, we saw hundreds of eager villagers crowded together awaiting our arrival. The people were hungry and had little clothing, but they are able to smile in appreciation as we began to unload the boxes of food. From the youngest to the oldest, outstretched hands reached out for their portion of

Wings of Health *takes off on another mercy flight*

food. Continuing through the afternoon, we finally distributed the last bit of supplies. We then decided to drive to another village that appeared to have been in the path of the lava flow.

Passing by the airport to reach the village, I was alarmed to see that the winds had shifted and were now sending ash in the direction where our airplane was parked. I realized we must act quickly and turned immediately into the airport. The PAL flight had already departed, and radioing my intentions, I was soon given permission to take off without the normal departure procedure. Once airborne, I turned to miss the dense and falling ash directly in front of me. We were close . . . very close and I breathed a prayer of thankfulness as we flew beyond the eruption to clear skies and a safe return to Manila.

Although we were not able to reach the village, our decision to travel to yet another area of need alerted us to the danger at the airport. I had kept frequently informed throughout the afternoon, but this had been a very sudden and unexpected shift in the winds. Had we not passed by the airport at that exact moment, we would not have discovered the change occurring which would have been a serious threat to our aircraft.

Later, as the ash lessened and the eruption subsided, we made additional flights to other areas hit hard by the eruption. How grateful I was for an airplane and for ADRA to be able to respond to this tragic call for help.

A divine design—Health Expo evangelism

Standing in the Rizal Memorial Arena in Manila, I stared at seventeen thousand seats. *Just what am I going to do?* I wondered. I had been asked to plan a health attraction for those attending Pastor Neal Wilson's evangelistic meetings. My husband would be presenting the health lecture each evening and the planning committee felt there should be some event for the guests when they first arrived. As I walked around the lower level of the arena, the challenge appeared overwhelming. *What would interest and accommodate large crowds like this?* I wondered, praying for guidance. While contemplating just what could be done, a sudden thought came to mind: the World's Fair with all its colorful exhibits.

Why not present our health message in similar appealing exhibits, one exhibit for each of the eight principles of health?[2] The exhibits could include short lectures and demonstrations on various topics of health, as well as health screening and counseling. The idea seemed divinely inspired. "Write the vision and make it plain upon tables." Yes, the text, Habakkuk 2:2, was a familiar one to me. I left the arena that day feeling confident that the Lord had given me a direct answer to my prayer.

The next morning I had been invited to speak for worship at the Manila Sanitarium and Hospital. As I was preparing for my talk early that morning, my eyes fell upon a verse in Esther, "For who knoweth whether thou are come to the kingdom for such a time as this?" (4:14). I seemed to read into it "to Manila for such a time as this." I presented this challenge to the workers later that morning. The response was immediate. The staff—both medical and nonmedical—were willing to participate in the program, which I decided to call "Health Expo."

Pastor Jim Zachary was a great help in preparing the plywood frames for the exhibits. Artists painted directly onto the plywood panels as I sketched the layout, text, and drawings for each one. Text and illustrations all had to be hand drawn, and I knew beyond a doubt that it was the Lord who enabled our team to finish

---

2. Nutrition, Exercise, Water, Sunshine, Temperance, Air, Rest, and Trust in Divine Power.

Anna and Lena with patient, Kenny, in Russian Health Expo.

all of the paintings in time for the opening meeting. I was grateful to have been able to find artists, including one who had the use of only one hand, for the project. I believe God must have provided the extra hand for this conscientious young artist as he was able to do as much as those with two hands! Because of the size of the arena and the expected number of guests, we felt additional exhibits were needed. When completed, there were three panels for each exhibit, with two exhibits on each theme, making a total of forty-eight panels and sixteen exhibits.

Crowds packed into the exhibits and the arena that first night. Upon entering the arena, one of the pastors from the overseas team exclaimed in astonishment, "What's going on here? I thought this was an evangelistic meeting. It looks more like a three-ring circus!" He was unaware of the plan to use exhibits and as he stood watching the milling crowds, I invited him to take a tour of the exhibits. As we walked past the exercise exhibit, I asked if he would like his blood pressure checked. "Well, it must be pretty high right now," he responded.

We continued on to the water exhibit where a hot foot bath was being demonstrated. In the air exhibit was a youthful crowd all attracted by the lung function test. Completing the tour of all eight exhibits, we passed by the nutrition exhibit once again where tasty samples were attracting a large crowd. Pausing with a serious look on his face, the pastor remarked, "Dorothy, why haven't we been doing this all along? This is what evangelism is all about."

We thanked the Lord for this little seed planted in Manila and which later was carried through the ministry of the *Wings of Health* aircraft to many other islands of the Philippines. Yes, with the Lord's blessing, the Health Expo program has continued and reached more than forty countries and several hundred cities. The exhibit panels have been translated into several dozen languages including Chinese, Russian, Hungarian, Uzbek, Farci, Karakalpak, Tajik, Kyrgyz, Turkmen, Korean, with the latest in Arabic to name a few. The panels have been prepared and printed by my son, Ken, following translation. The Health Expo concept has been used in overseas programs by The Quiet Hour, OCI (Outpost Centers International), It Is Written, The Voice of Prophecy and various other organizations and churches. How I thank the Lord for this divinely appointed plan of evangelism . . . a wonderful answer to prayer not only for Manila but for the world.

"The little seed planted that day in Manila resulted in sixty Health Expos in Russia. What a blessing to have had this opportunity . . . not only were we blessed with two excellent young translators—they eventually became our two new daughters-in-law!"

Angel wings over the *Wings of Health*

"The typhoon has changed course with the eye of the storm heading directly toward the island of Cebu," a voice on Radio

Cebu announced. It was the latest alert. This storm warning was not unusual, as typhoons frequently plague the Philippine islands. Typhoon Nitang (Ike), however, with winds over 100 miles per hour, was now heading directly toward Cebu where the *Wings of Health* airplane was parked. Without the security of a hangar, we were very concerned and quickly drove out to the airport to see how we could secure the airplane.

Upon our arrival, we noticed that many of the lighter aircraft were turned and facing a particular direction. In studying the path of the typhoon and wind currents, however, I concluded that the aircraft should be turned in the opposite direction. With the use of sandbags, we secured the plane, and then, in special prayer with our mission president, Pastor Niere, who had joined us, we placed the *Wings of Health* in the care of our heavenly Father.

During the night, we were awakened with the sense that we should pray again. It was midnight and the winds were blowing with alarming and unbelievable force. Trees were falling around us and we braced our windows with mattresses. *Oh, Lord, please protect the airplane—your airplane. We know without your intervention the* Wings of Health *will not survive!* We were experiencing the most severe and dangerous typhoon ever to hit Cebu.

At the break of dawn, we hurried to look out the window where our mattresses had fortunately held firm. What we saw was a war zone! Fallen trees covered houses and debris blocked the streets. Power lines were down, roofs of houses had been swept away, and cars were badly damaged. *How will we ever get through to the airport?* I wondered. We wanted desperately to check on the *Wings of Health* airplane but the roads were impassable. Later in the morning, work crews began clearing the roads and eventually Bill and I were able to drive around the debris to reach the airport.

Our airplane could not have possibly survived without a miracle, I thought, my heart heavy as I surveyed the damage along our route. We are soon within sight of the airport and our eyes strained for a glimpse of the plane. The roof of the building which housed the Flight Service Station had been torn away. There was extensive damage to buildings and airplanes alike.

And then looking directly ahead we see it . . . the *Wings of Health,* its wings glistening from the sun's rays . . . unmoved and untouched . . . standing as a witness to God's care and answered prayer. How we praised our heavenly Father! God's angels must have surrounded the aircraft that frightful and terrible night. General Singson from the Philippine Air Force came over to look at the miracle aircraft untouched by the fury of one of the most severe typhoons ever to hit the island. Tragically, there were 1,363 deaths reported in the areas of Cebu, Surigao, Bohol, and Negros.

CHAPTER 14
The Greatest Air Event of All Times

It's my sincere belief that most pilots feel a bit closer to heaven than their earthbound counterparts. I'm sure that many of them have expressed sheer delight and thrill at that first takeoff as they began flying lessons. What pilot doesn't continue to feel emotion when hearing the words, "Cleared for takeoff?" I know I can never forget my first lesson at a little airport in Collegedale, Tennessee.

Taxiing onto the runway, the instructor suddenly told me to take the controls of the little red *Cessna 150* and just "take off!" I was a bit surprised, but with a little prompting, I slowly pushed in the power and gently pulled back on the yoke at the speed the instructor told me. What an exciting moment it was. I was leaving the ground. I was in the air. I was flying! A childhood dream was coming true. Even today I still feel that excitement in hearing the words, "Cleared for takeoff."

As a child swinging in our old cherry tree, I would stretch my legs higher and higher, trying to touch the tip of a cloud with my toes. *If only on the "up swing" I can keep going,* I wished, and so I would pump even harder. *Could it happen?* I wondered. But the old tire swing could only tempt me to dream on.

Who hasn't thought of a flight to the great beyond? Many of us have dreamed the impossible and now those dreams are coming true. Man cannot only fly to the moon, he can walk on the moon. Man now swings into *orbit,* and not simply from an old cherry tree.

Pilots are a special group, and as Neil Armstrong, Commander of *Apollo 11,* once told the world while walking on the moon: "One small step for [a] man. One giant leap for mankind." Another astronaut, James Irwin, when thrust into space and watching the earth diminish in size, exclaimed, "Seeing this has to change a man, has to make a man appreciate the creation of God." I believe that many astronauts, pilots, and even passengers in airplanes recognize the Creator in the great "up there." It's not just a child trying to touch the clouds, not even an astronaut walking on the moon, but all of mankind fulfilling a dream. It is a dream to someday fly weightless through space, to visit other planets without the need of Houston Control, shuttles, space suits, space stations, or weather briefings. Our Commander-in-Chief has taken care of it all.

Who hasn't been thrilled to watch the Blue Angels and other aircraft flying in close formation? Who hasn't become breathless in seeing the incredible maneuvers of jet aircraft flying heavenward? There seems to be just no equal to the thrill of an air show. This coming air event, however, will be different. We do not need to remain on the ground as spectators. We can be participants. The good news is that all can be part of the greatest air event; all who choose can be a part of this once-in-a-lifetime experience.

The best news is that this flight is already planned and is currently in a holding pattern, waiting for all passengers who choose to board. It's a confirmed flight and when our Commander clears us for "takeoff," it will be seven days of sheer delight flying through space along with thousands of other passengers, tens of thousands of angels, and our Commander-in-Chief who is leading the flight. Our destination: the Celestial City, Heaven itself. As we wing our way and glide to a touchdown on the "Sea of Glass," we will hear a voice which resounds through the vast multitudes and the entire universe.

"Welcome home, children!" It is the voice of our Commander-in-Chief, our loving heavenly Father. He is waiting to bestow on all of us our certificates, our emblems of victory. Each passenger is listed and accounted for in a logbook. From one pilot who is preparing to be on that flight, my radio message is loud and clear, "Get ready, get set for flight." All pilots, would-be pilots, and passengers young and old, will not want to miss the greatest air event of all times. Our Commander-in-Chief is coming "in the clouds of heaven with power and great glory. And he shall send his angels with a great sound of a trumpet, and they shall gather together his elect from the four winds, from one end of heaven to the other" (Matthew 24:30, 31). He will soon give the command "Cleared for takeoff!" All who choose, all who believe can be on that passenger list. How about it, pilot friend, and all the rest of those who have ever dreamed that someday they might fly? The Owner's Manual has already confirmed the flight. Let's not miss out on this greatest air event of all times!

"Behold, he cometh with clouds; and every eye shall see him" (Revelation 1:7).

Epilogue

The *Lake Amphibian* went down because of a mechanic's faulty installation of a quick drain in Portland, Maine, causing the loss of all the oil. The insurance company covered the cost of the aircraft after a thorough inspection of the maintenance records and pilot logbooks. The insurance company initially thought that it was some type of planned publicity event since the aircraft touched down in the only place within a hundred miles it could land safely.

The helicopter pilots who rescued us agreed to airlift the *Lake Amphibian* to a place where another engine could be installed. Unfortunately, because of the delay with the insurance company to confirm my "unbelievable story," they found the aircraft had already broken up and drifted sixteen miles south.

In contacting the FAA as to how to report the loss, I was told by a representative, "In our books, we consider Lake 1107 Lima nothing less than a miracle." The official records simply state "unknown" as to what happened to the aircraft. Of course, there are those who do know what happened to the aircraft but for those who don't know I share this remarkable experience. It's an experience filled with miracles . . . batteries that don't freeze so communication can be maintained, an ice storm that stops suddenly when usually lasting five to seven days, a touchdown made in the only possible place within a hundred miles to land safely, a night on twelve inches of ice in subzero temperatures without frost bite or possible polar bear attack. These are nothing less than miracles . . . miracles that two pilots know beyond a doubt had divine intervention.

"My eternal thanks to the One who made it all possible."

"I feel there is no conflict between the natural feelings of fear in a crisis and one's personal faith. Pilots . . . mission pilots constantly face dangers as has been my experience in the primitive and rebel infiltrated areas into which I have flown. I believe as they do that God is directing our lives and feel confident that those who have fallen in sacrificial service will one day fly again!"

ABOUT THE AUTHOR

Dorothy Nelson spent twenty years as missionary teacher in the Far East (Taiwan and Hong Kong) with her husband, Wilbur. She served as chairman of the Department of Nursing at South China Union College, and professor of music at the Taiwan Academy of Fine Arts. She was the coeditor of the Chinese Hymnal and an author of Ellen White books for children.

Dorothy received a BA degree from La Sierra College with Master's Degrees in Public Health (Loma Linda University) and Music (Claremont University); she is a registered nurse and pilot with commercial, instrument, multiengine land and sea, and flight instructor ratings. She served as pilot of the *Piper Aztec* and *Beech Twin Bonanza,* mission planes operated under Medical Aviation Programs, Inc. of the Philippines. Subsequently, she instructed in the *Twin Bonanza* and flew medical flights for physicians from Loma Linda University Medical Center.

She participated in the China project with It is Written, developing health awareness television infomercials that aired nationwide in China and was associated with The Quiet Hour as Health Expo coordinator for evangelism and mission pilot. Formerly director of Weimar Institute's NEWSTART® Outpatient Program/Health Expo Outreach and field representative, she is the founder and president of H.E.L.P. (Health Expo Lifestyle Programs). H.E.L.P has been used in global evangelism in some forty countries and three hundred cities. She currently conducts Wellness Weekends and coordinates Health Expo programs in various churches, as well as overseas missions (www.HealthExpo.org).

In addition to her service overseas, Dorothy developed a program in drug education for school children in California for which she received commendation from the Surgeon General on behalf of the President of the United States.

She has five children—two physician sons, Ken and Richard; a son, Lawrence, retired nurse and businessman; a daughter, Janet (Penner), teacher; and son, James, in the field of information security. Her late husband, Wilbur Nelson, PhD, DrPH, was formerly Professor of International Health at Loma Linda University, consultant with the Department of Health in the Philippines, and Health Education Consultant for the Western Pacific with the World Health Organization.

This book was completed while Dorothy was on teaching assignment in Riyadh where two of her sons, Richard and Ken, are faculty members of Loma Linda University—Saudi Arabia.

Acknowledgements

For the more than twenty physicians and surgeons who donated their time in treatments to nearly one thousand patients including one hundred surgeries . . . all at no cost . . . I am deeply grateful. MAP began with a small amount of funds, a plane, a pilot, a physician, and a large amount of faith! The program has seen remarkable growth, expanding from one small outdoor clinic on a forgotten island to fifteen clinics and a ten bed hospital. Hospitals who have opened their doors to medical and surgical cases included Manila Sanitarium and Hospital, Miller Sanitarium and Hospital (Cebu), Mindanao Sanitarium and Hospital (Iligan), Aurora Memorial Hospital (Baler), Ago General Hospital (Legaspi) and the Philippine Heart Center for Asia.

The Department of Health supplied medicines, and fuel was provided by the Philippine Air Force. We greatly appreciated the assistance of the Aw Boon Haw foundation and the visit of Sally Aw and Dr. P. H. Teng. Dr. Lloyd and Chris Griffith, both pilots, were a continuing support in the Health Expo programs. Dr. Griffith personally participated in reaching remote areas with his presentations on a healthy lifestyle.

A wide range of patients from newborn babies to the elderly were airlifted in the *Wings of Health* aircraft. Almost too numerous to mention, my flights included patients with leprosy, tuberculosis, hepatitis, malnutrition, goiter, pneumonias, harelip, cancer, heart disease, kidney stones, accidents, and blindness. To be able to airlift a patient, a child without hope and seemingly an inoperable condition to the hospital is oftentimes hard work. To return that young child, healed with a future again is the most enjoyable hard work I have ever experienced!

Those who inspired me in mission service . . . husband, Bill; the Harry Millers and my father, J. R. Nelson. Dr. Miller treated many Hakka boat people on the Robert's Sea-Light boat where this picture was taken.

Surgical team flown to Iligan.

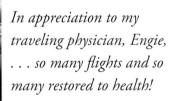

In appreciation to my traveling physician, Engie, . . . so many flights and so many restored to health!

Medical team

*Manila
Sanitarium and
Hospital team
on another
mercy flight*

*Dr. Lloyd and
Chris Griffith . . .
two missionary
minded team
members (both pilots) for giving invalu-
able service and support to our mission
activities. Their special involvement
and personal participation in Health
Expo evangelism programs has resulted
in changed lives around the world. The
EGW study guides by Chris Griffith are
well known and appreciated.*

*In appreciation to the late
Aubrey Kinzer for his
dedication to mission
aviation.*

If you enjoyed reading this book you want to read these also:

Shot Down!
John M. Curnow

After his bomber exploded, author John Curnow found himself riding a parachute into German-occupied France—his crew's sole survivor. It's said that in a POW camp, only 25 percent of the prisoners are interested in escaping, and only 5 percent are what is known as "dedicated escapers." He was one of those. Time and again he escaped his captors. But after each escape he found himself held captive again. After the war, bad habits and a fast-paced life going nowhere held him.

Then one day his arm seemed to be shackled. When his hand refused to turn off the quartet singing "Lift up the Trumpet" on the radio, he began to find his way to true, enduring freedom at last.

ISBN 10: 0-8163-2109-4 Paperback.

Amazing True Mission Stories
J. H. Zachary

Don't think miracles ended when the last of Jesus' disciples died. God is accomplishing amazing things on a daily basis around the world right now. You'll read about an army of bees that saved a church, an entire village that came to know Jesus because a mission pilot landed on "the wrong" airstrip. These and scores of other true mission stories will inspire you.

ISBN 10: 0-8163-1982-0 Paperback.

More Amazing True Mission Stories
J. H. and Jean Zachary

When great missionaries die, their work lives on. So do their stories. James H. Zachary did not live to see this second book of true stories published. But with the help of his dear wife Jean, James still testifies to a miracle-working God in this second collection of amazing true mission stories.

ISBN 10: 0-8163-2079-9 Paperback.

Three ways to order:

1 Local	Adventist Book Center®	
2 Call	1-800-765-6955	
3 Shop	AdventistBookCenter.com	

 **Pacific Press**®